Praise for the Vissells

"I can't think of anything more important to the healing of our society than a connection between spirituality, relationship, and parenthood. Bravo to the Vissells for helping us find the way."
>—**Marianne Williamson**, author of *A Return to Love*

"Barry and Joyce plow through the hard and soft spaces of the journey with great inner strength and deep respect for reflective inner tuning."
>—**Ram Dass**, author of *Be Here Now*

"We highly recommend *The Heart's Wisdom* to anyone who values clarity, honesty, and growth in their relationships. This book is inspiring, powerful, and liberating."
>—**John Robbins**, author of *Diet for a New America*

"I convey my best wishes to you both for the important work you are doing."
>—**Al Gore**, Vice President of the United States

"It is so refreshing to see a wife and husband team writing books and teaching workshops on relationship as a deeply united and committed couple. Their work goes straight to the heart."
>—**Geneen Roth**, author of *When Food Is Love*

"We have always benefited from the gentle wisdom of the Vissells. *The Heart's Wisdom* is one of the rare voices for sanity in the field of relationships."
>—**Gayle and Hugh Prather**, authors of *I Will Never Leave You*

"The Vissells' work will bless your whole life."
>—**John Bradshaw**, author of *Healing the Shame That Binds You*

THE Heart's Wisdom

A Practical Guide to Growing Through Love

JOYCE & BARRY VISSELL

FOREWORD BY
HUGH AND GAYLE PRATHER

CONARI PRESS
Berkeley, California

Conari Press books are distributed by Publishers Group West

A previous edition of this work was published under
the title *Light in the Mirror*

Words and music by Libby Roderick © 1988 Libby Roderick Music.
From the recording *If You See a Dream*. Available through
Turtle Island Records, (907) 278-6817

ISBN: 1-57324-155-5

Cover Photography: Images copyright © 1998 PhotoDisc, Inc.
Book cover and interior design: Suzanne Albertson
Cover art direction: Ame Beanland

Library of Congress Cataloging-in-Publication Data

Vissell, Joyce.
The heart's wisdom : a practical guide to growing through love /
Joyce & Barry Vissell : foreword by Hugh and Gayle Prather.
p.   cm.
ISBN 1-57324-155-5 (tradepaper)
1. Spiritual life—New Age movement. 2. Interpersonal relationships—
Religious aspects—New Age movement. I. Vissell. Barry.
II. Title.
BP605.N48V585 1999   99-11549
299'.93—dc21   CIP

Printed in the United States of America on recycled paper
99 00 01 02   RRD H   10 9 8 7 6 5 4 3 2 1

We dedicate this book to our children, Rami, Mira, and John-Nuriel, who have shown us a reflection of unconditional love and acceptance. We trust we have done the same for them.

What you are looking for is who is looking.

—Saint Francis

Foreword

Barry and Joyce: The Gentle Teachers
A Foreword by Hugh and Gayle Prather

AS YOU READ THIS BOOK, YOU WILL BE IN GOOD HANDS. We have had a close relationship with Joyce and Barry Vissell for many years. They have three kids. We have three kids. They have made mistakes in their marriage. We have made even more mistakes in ours. Throughout the years, the four of us have compared notes about our children, our finances, our marriages, our spiritual efforts, and our love of God. We have done this so many times that we can assure you that Barry and Joyce have hearts of gold and insights of pure light.

Of all the Vissells' great strengths as teachers, possibly their greatest is their ability to focus attention directly on what is blocking a couple's awareness of the love between them. A spiritual approach to relationship begins with the recognition that all hearts are connected. Unity is a preexisting state. In most relationship books, the couple is instructed how to put in place what is not there. The couple's task is to rebuild what has been lost or to create what was lacking from the beginning.

The difficulty with this approach is that the two individuals are alone in their responsibility for the amount of love between them. At any juncture, should one partner's efforts falter, the relationship is instantly diminished, and the only remedy is for that person to get back up to speed. Within this model, love is like two people who hold a rope between them, feeling their way in the dark. If one person's grip loosens, their connection ends, and they both are lost to a love-less night.

The Vissells see clearly that because we all carry each other in our hearts, the correction to any mistake we may have made is already within us. We have not been left alone to solve the impossible dilemma of how to make two individuals—who are in all respects dif-ferent—united. To the contrary, we are surrounded at all times by unlimited help, and any effort we make to love our partner, no mat-ter how slight, is supported by Love itself and all the host of heaven.

But the Vissells do not stop there. They don't leave couples with mere spiritual truisms to battle the little hells in which they continu-ally find themselves. The Vissells vigorously point out exactly how couples blind themselves to the fact that they already love each other, and they provide the simple steps needed to erase the blind spots.

Closeness—the feeling of enjoying each other, the feeling of rest and peace in each other's presence—does not have to be created. Unity is our divine inheritance. All we need do is remove what blocks our awareness of it. Love is the recognition of the familiar within each other. It is experiencing how we are the same and feeling this same-ness. But to do that we have to look unflinchingly at our partner's imperfections and at our own. It is not by denying our partner's shadow side that we see the light of his or her heart. Those who try to whip up positive feelings merely by adding spiritual concepts to their churning egos will accomplish nothing permanent.

What we already believe about ourselves and our partner must be seen and accepted. Each dark thought must be looked at calmly. Then our vision can move naturally to our deeper perceptions. The good-ness of the heart is already in place. Nothing has to be done about it. The key to oneness is not verbally affirming the divine in our partner. It is seeing and accepting our partner's ego and our own. Once we see our demons in detail, they lose their power to block our vision of the heart's goodness.

The Vissells point out that there are no perfect partners and there are no perfect children. Each of us has a doubting mind. Couples who have made it to what Joyce and Barry call "the third stage" are not sterling human beings. They are ordinary people who have seen, accepted, and are comfortable with their ordinariness. They know each other's foibles well and are at ease. "If the same thought (of doubt) comes over and over, look at it carefully. . ." say the Vissells. "Every good gardener knows the importance of plucking out the weeds as they come."

You simply can't see the perfection, the just-right-ness, of your partner as long as you are denying that your partner has an ego. Your vision will stop cold at any layer of denial. If you feel judgmental of your partner, you can be sure that you are denying that you are both alike, that you are gardens capable of producing both flowers and weeds. The instant you are comfortable with your partner's ego thoughts—because you recognize that you too have ego thoughts— you begin to see the relationship that was always there, that always embraced you both. Now you need no words to evoke the divine, because you are already a part of it.

Hugh and Gayle Prather, ministers and authors of *Spiritual Parenting; I Will Never Leave You; and Spiritual Notes to Myself.*

1

Our Life's Assignment

The only thing you have to offer another human being, ever, is your own state of being.

—RAM DASS

HILE WE WERE WRITING THIS BOOK, we sometimes wished we could travel to a mountaintop and focus entirely on our writing. If we could only remove ourselves from the activity of our day-to-day lives, we reasoned, we could more clearly write our deepest feelings about living from the heart.

It never happened. Our three children—eighteen-year-old Rami, thirteen-year-old Mira, and five-year-old John-Nuriel—each needed us in their own way. In addition, our commitment to helping others and our financial responsibilities (we built a new home and center) could not be abandoned. So, writing this book had to be juggled among homework needs, running a nonprofit, public service organization, play rehearsals, counseling clients, before-school meetings, games of Uno, getting a young adult ready for college, hide and seek, and travel all over the country to conduct workshops. Sometimes we couldn't resist envying other authors who could focus entirely on their writing.

In the final stages, however, we realized that working on the book in the midst of home, family, and service responsibilities has given our writing a special quality. We didn't need to leave our involvement with the world in order to feel love within ourselves and for one another. Instead, we realized the highest spirituality is attained through loving ourselves and one another in the midst of all the interruptions and responsibilities of everyday life. Learning our true purpose here on Earth—completing our soul assignment, if you will—requires our willingness to behold two things: the beauty of our loved ones and of all beings and things outside us *and* the beauty of our own being reflected back from the great mirror of life.

As the two of us have traveled throughout the country sharing our work, we have often heard people describe the same spiritual longing—a longing for deeper connection not only with other people but with their own hearts as well. Many of the people we have met are trying to connect more deeply with themselves and with others. Regardless of whether they are single or a couple, they are searching for spiritual meaning in their lives and a deeper sense of peace within themselves.

We have met some people who, in their efforts to reach God, the light of all creation, have avoided intimate relationships altogether. They believe the only way to attain true spiritual awakening is by shunning the world and its complexities. Often, these people are convinced that by remaining single and solitary, they are coming closer to the highest spiritual awareness. In addition, we have met many couples who are experiencing difficulty in their relationship and who seriously doubt that being in relationship can possibly enhance their spiritual growth.

Indeed, throughout the course of history, spirituality was often kept separate from relationships. Individuals following a spiritual discipline often felt they needed to stay away from relationships in order to awaken. In their minds, a relationship was thought to be a "worldly" activity, a departure from the spiritual path.

Through our own joining—a journey of thirty-five years so far—we have learned something very different about the nature of spiritual awakening and relationships. We believe that the essence of every individual is a vast spiritual energy, a radiant light that is helping us to grow and unfold the petals of a magnificent flower. That flower, that magnificent inner light, *is* us—our real identity. It is only by knowing this deepest part of ourselves that we can acquire true wisdom, true happiness, and "the peace that passes all understanding."

In addition, we have learned that the process of joining with another can be a sacred path. Far from being an obstacle to our spiritual development, relationships can actually be catalysts for the unfolding of the flower of ourselves. Walking the path of relationship deepens the soul's capacity for compassion and the heart's capacity for embracing love, and helps us to understand love's cycles of giving and receiving. The closer we come to another, the better we come to know ourselves, and, in so doing, the closer we come to God, the ever-present light and love within and all around us.

In this book, you may find many new ideas, but to us they're not new at all—they're as old as love itself. Unfortunately, much of the wisdom about loving has simply been lost in our culture. We have written this book to reclaim that lost wisdom, and we hope to help it root once again in our present-day world.

One of the ideas at the heart of this book that may seem new to some readers is the image of relationship as a soul mirror. Through this metaphor, we hope to show people how *every* relationship—no matter its duration or configuration—is a mirror in which they can see and understand the deeper, hidden parts of themselves. No one can grow spiritually without introspection, a journey inside themselves. A mirror is a device for looking at ourselves, for seeing the parts of ourselves that are difficult, if not impossible, to see without this help. Every relationship offers us just such a reflection of ourselves, if we are willing to look, and learn, and grow. Yet more than merely showing us our defects and shortcomings, and how we need to grow, the mirror of relationship can, more important, help us see our own beauty and lovability. Through the process of loving and being loved in return, we can reclaim our true spiritual greatness.

THE PATH'S THREE PHASES

We have learned that the path of spiritual awakening and the path of relationship have much in common. Each has three main phases. The first is the "heavenly glimpse." Whether it be a glimpse of the light of God (within us) or a glimpse of the light of a lover (outside us), we have a momentary view of the same light. It is just as uplifting to see the light within our own heart as it is to see the light within the heart of our beloved. This first phase is the "honeymoon" phase, complete with its thrill of newness and the excitement of discovery.

The second phase of both spiritual and relationship awakening is the journey past the obstacles that stand in the way of love. The "honeymoon" is over (although elements of its newness can be felt from time to time), and this is the time to learn the many necessary lessons about life and love. On the personal spiritual path, it is the time when we confront the dark side of our personality, the parts of us that rob us of our peace. On the path of relationship, it is the time when we illuminate the interaction between our own and our partner's dark sides.

The third phase of the spiritual and relationship path is service. As our cup fills with love, our natural desire is to give from overflow, to offer joyfully to the world the love and the help we ourselves have received. Service is sharing the fruits of our personal spiritual growth and our relationship.

Furthermore, the spiritual and relationship journeys are not linear, one phase following the next. All three phases can be happening at the same time. Serving and helping others can teach us even more lessons about unconditional love, which, in turn, can create more newness and "honeymoon-like" joy. In addition, all of evolution follows an upward spiral. We may seem to go full circle, ending up in a similar place to where we began, but we are never in the same place.

We are on the next level of the spiral, perhaps near the old place, but with more understanding and wisdom.

We have written *The Heart's Wisdom* as a kind of guidebook to help you integrate these two paths, the path of spiritual growth and the path of relationship. Throughout the book, we hope we have made it clear that these two paths continually overlap, that your personal spiritual growth enriches your relationships and your relationships enrich your spiritual awakening. Although the two of us have been in a very long-term committed relationship, we believe this book can be helpful for anyone, no matter what your relationship circumstance. Single, married, divorced, dating, looking for that special someone, we are always in relationship—to ourselves and with those around us.

One of our greatest hopes is that this book can help you to learn to accept and love all the parts of yourself and to embrace all the soul lessons of life and relationship.

2

Lovers from Before

Lovers do not meet somewhere along the way.
They're in each other's hearts from the beginning.

—RUMI

THE RELATIONSHIP BETWEEN BARRY AND ME seemed to begin before we met at age eighteen. It had been one of the main themes of my childhood play and fantasy: to reunite with my beloved. By the time we met, it felt like we had been in love our whole lives.

I remember as a child being sent to my room when I was crying or upset. Perhaps my parents were trying to understand my feelings, but in my young mind and heart I felt alone. I remember so clearly how, during one of those times, I heard an inner voice speak to me. I had never had this experience before and listened carefully to the message. It told me that when I was grown, I would meet a man who would understand my feelings, that I would recognize him as a tall, dark-haired doctor who would become my best friend. From early childhood, I trusted this message, which came to me over and over again whenever I felt that no one understood me.

Barry and I found each other in a clumsy, youthful way. I remember, when I met Barry during my first year in college, the surge of energy that shot through me when he told me he was a premedical student. We eyed each other with mixed feelings. Neither one of us felt particularly attracted to the other's appearance, yet we could not deny an energy that flowed between us.

Two days after we met, we had our first date to see a movie. We hurried back to my college dorm to meet the curfew time. Mrs. Peabody, the elderly dorm mother, was waiting by the glass door.

"You have two minutes to get inside," she snapped at me and continued to peer through the glass.

Oblivious to Mrs. Peabody's stern observation, we kissed for the first time. In that moment, a door to another world flew open, and it was as if we recognized one another. Standing in a daze, I heard Mrs. Peabody open the door. She pulled me inside and shut the door on Barry.

That kiss changed my life forever. Our young hearts were hardly ready for the power of our connection, but our first kiss revealed a love that seemed to have existed for eternity. Barry, my tall, skinny, awkward eighteen-year-old boyfriend, really seemed to be my beloved for all time past and all time to come. We had found each other and yet couldn't fully comprehend the blessing. I feel so much gratitude to have found Barry so early in life and to still be living with him.

Many religions hold sacred the belief that lovers have known each other before coming into this world, and will know each other again—that our loving has a purpose far beyond the limitations of our own understanding.

Over the years, the following image has often come to me, so vivid I believe it must be a memory: *I can remember being in a circle of many souls. Barry and I are apart from each other. There is a great love and union among all of these souls. We are under the guidance of great light and spiritual energy, and are preparing to come to Earth. Each one is being given an assignment or gift to give while on Earth. Each is called upon and asked to spread the light and love of God in various ways. Barry and I are called up simultaneously and asked to work together to help bring more light into human relationships. We feel deep love for each other and for our Creator. Our purpose on Earth is blessed by the light, and we are given one instruction: Love one another completely and let that love overflow to others in healing and guidance. There are other souls given the same assignment. We know that all the help we need will come from our contact with the light.*

Barry and I feel that this light is present in all heart connections. We understand that the highest work we can do is to love one another completely, but there are times when our egos cringe at having to be together. Each of us has had moments when we have wanted to give up on our relationship and just be alone. We also have lessons to learn and personalities that sometimes clash and cause each other pain. We've had to do much work on our relationship and have much more to do. Sometimes we both wish our relationship could be a little easier. As with many people, our minds seek the easy way out. However, our hearts, which hold the vision of our purpose together, seek to be with someone who will help each of us on our spiritual journey, no matter how difficult.

We believe the lesson for others in our story is this: When looking for your spiritual partner, for the relationship that has already been blessed in "heaven," keep your heart open. Your partner may not appear to be what your mind thinks it wants. You may be in for a big surprise! If you are listening in your heart, you will recognize your partner. If you listen to your head about what you want, you may miss this special person altogether.

After our first kiss, Barry and I set out to get to know each other. We figured out a way to avoid the scrutiny of Mrs. Peabody. We'd meet in the cafeteria, and I would come back to my room through the basement. We realized we were breaking the rules, but there was just too much to talk about. Barry told me all the most embarrassing, shameful, and confusing times of his life—all in our second conversation! There was a comfort in talking to one another that neither of us had ever experienced. A pressure was released as we shared everything that had happened in the eighteen years we had been on Earth. Everything was met with love and acceptance. We felt so much at home.

Then came the evening Barry told me he was Jewish. It was such a shock! I had assumed he was Protestant like me, since we were both going to Hartwick College, a small Protestant school. He had assumed that my last name, Wollenberg, was Jewish. This revelation saddened us and brought us to the realization that we could never marry. We would have to "just be friends." Before, our hearts were opening in love to each other. Now, with the news of our different religions, our minds began to take over to protect ourselves from the seemingly inevitable loss, because we each felt we could never marry outside our religion. At that time, in 1964, it seemed an insurmountable obstacle. Our hearts even then felt they had found the perfect spiritual partner. Our minds, however, were already rejecting each other because of our different religions. Still, our lips kept finding their way together and thus helped to bring us back to the awareness of our spiritual union and purpose together.

The first four years of our relationship were a bittersweet mixture of love and confusion. Between the many attempts to free ourselves from each other, there was, nevertheless, a deepening of love and respect, as well as the powerful physical passion of our youth. Attempts to rid ourselves of each other were as useless as trying to change our own reflections in the mirror. So we kept returning to the embrace of lovers.

Once we realized how difficult it would be to separate from one another, our scheming minds planned strategies that would change each other to fit our own pictures of the perfect partner. However, we were (and are) both much too stubborn; any effort to change the other was met with resistance and even hostility. Finally, there was one thing left to do: we gave up our minds' ideas of how the other should change. Fortunately for us, our hearts won over our minds. Barry and I accepted each other, differences and all, and were married on December 21, 1968. We feel our wedding was simply a reenactment of the union in my heavenly memories. Though we were in the early stages of spiritual awakening, we each felt a strong presence of light blessing us. The tears in our eyes during the ceremony seemed to wash away the veil that hid the deep memory of our prior union and blessing.

We are now devoted to remembering our connection and serving others through that love. We have a distance to go and the dedication to go there. Each time someone is helped by our words or by our work, it helps us more strongly to remember our purpose. Each time our relationship becomes bogged down, yet we break through to renewed love, we realize we are giving a gift to others. Our love for one another and for the "assignment" we have been given is the top priority in our lives. We believe in the beauty of all relationships and in the great light that brings two souls together.

If, in your heart, there is a desire to have a spiritual partner, then you are feeling what is already in your destiny, what is already in a plan bigger than anything your mind can conceive. You may find this person when you are young, or you may find him or her later in life, when perhaps you have had several other relationships. Whenever you find this person, treasure him or her with all your heart. This soul mirror has been given to you to help you fulfill your purpose on Earth. Loving this one through both the easy and the difficult times will bring you fulfillment and love at the deepest level of your being.

The Vision of Our Work

Bringing our highest vision of spirituality into our work was a challenge in the beginning. Even before we married, each of us knew we wanted to help others. Eventually, Barry went into medical school and I began a career in nursing. We fully immersed ourselves in medicine for the first four years of our marriage, becoming competent, yet we knew something was missing. A feeling of the "heart" was lacking in our work.

Subsequently, I specialized in child psychiatry and Barry in adult psychiatry. While Barry was training, I practiced play therapy with children in the same department and trained medical students and doctors to work with children. We both had the opportunity to train in a variety of holistic therapy techniques, a welcome relief from the more highly structured medical model of traditional psychiatry. By the end of that period of time, we felt we were ready to begin the work we had come here to do. We knew we wanted to work together, helping people in the area of relationship.

In 1973, we led our first therapy group. In many ways it went well. There were powerful and touching moments, but we became painfully aware that there still was something missing—a more consistent heart-centered feeling. We were still too cerebral, too dependent on the methods we had learned—even the holistic ones. These methods weren't taking us to the deep places of understanding and healing, places we had always intuitively sensed. We knew we could never be satisfied until we learned how to bring the quality of the heart into our work with others. We realized the training we now needed was different from anything we had previously received.

So, while our friends and colleagues were setting up lucrative practices and getting on with their careers, we "dropped out" altogether. We equipped our VW bus for extended travel, stored our meager possessions, withdrew all the money we had scrimped and saved, and set out on what turned out to be a two-year "quest for the heart."

We turned to the Eastern practice of yoga, to allow our bodies to become more flexible and to tap into higher, more spiritual dimensions. We learned techniques to still our restless minds. Beginning our study of meditation with twenty minutes twice a day of transcendental meditation, we soon dove headlong into a ten-day Buddhist Vipassana meditation course, alternating between sitting and walking practices from early morning to late at night. By the end of that ten days, we understood the benefits a quiet mind brought to every part of our lives.

Delving into Sufism, as well as the inner, esoteric principles of our own heritage, Judaism and Christianity, we practiced methods of opening and centering in the heart—cultivating feelings of love, devotion, and compassion. We hungrily sought the essence of love from each tradition we encountered. Whenever a spiritual teacher was recommended, we traveled to meet them. We met some beautiful teachers and also a host of characters. We tried to learn from everyone we met.

We learned about the light that fills and surrounds all of creation and that seems to be a central part of most, if not all, religions and spiritual traditions. Especially in our deeper meditations, we experienced this light as the basis of all spirituality, as the very core and substance of God. With each experience of the light, whether visualized in our inner sight or felt as a warmth in our bodies, we were raised to a higher awareness and discovered a deeper peace and happiness. Consciously entering this light, whether in the stillness of meditation or during everyday living, produced a welling up of love within our hearts, a feeling of well-being and an acceptance of what is, rather than what should be.

At the end of two years, Barry and I were enjoying meditation. We had learned a wide variety of spiritual practices and met many sincere seekers and teachers. We were privileged to have a close and personal relationship with Leo Buscaglia, Ram Dass, Pir Vilayat Khan, Pearl Dorris, Hari Das Baba, Ylana Hayward, and Joan Hodgson from the White Eagle Lodge in England, and others. Each, in their own way, pointed us in the direction of the light. Each revealed to us the top of the same mountain, with many paths converging to the same point on top. We saw how, on each path at the bottom of the mountain, it was difficult to see the other paths. The paths were separated by more distance, and the mountaintop itself was often obscured from sight. As we climbed higher along each path, however, the goal came more frequently into sight—and it was possible to see more and more of the other paths all converging on the same peak.

After our pilgrimage, and ready to establish a home base to begin our work, we moved to Santa Cruz, California, and set up our second group. This was a marked improvement from our first one. We meditated and prayed at the beginning of each session, so that the sessions started out in a heartfelt way. Yet as we started working with a person, this would subtly change. Our psychiatry and psychology training would take over, and we'd be back in the area of the mind. In addition, when emotions such as sadness and anger would be expressed, we'd get lost and stuck in them, not knowing how to raise the emotional energy to include a heart and spiritual perspective. We would start out in the heart and swiftly move to a mind-centered psychological perspective—and stay there.

After half a year of facilitating groups, we still felt dissatisfied. We realized we didn't know how to stay "connected" to our hearts. It seemed clear that no individual or relationship could grow or heal if the heart or soul, the deepest places of truth, were ignored in the process. We remembered our original vision and inspiration to help people with their lives and their relationships, we felt our work was meant to be heart-centered, and yet we didn't know how to sustain that energy.

Our culture glorifies the mind. Yet real wisdom can only be found in a much deeper place within us, the heart. The heart holds the feeling of expansive openness and love and, therefore, the feeling of real power. The mind can be a great tool, but it can also seek control in the guise of power. The heart is already powerful and intuitively knowing, so it has no need to control anything.

We decided to stop doing groups altogether and to concentrate instead on living from our hearts. This period of time turned out to be seven years. During this time, we simplified our lives and finances enormously. We lived isolated in the country. Our priority became living from the heart and listening to our intuition. While doctor friends were becoming well established in their careers, Barry was working as little as possible to get by and earning a doctor's minimum wage in an assortment of clinics. At home, aside from a sporadic counseling practice, we concentrated fully on integrating what we knew intellectually with what we felt in the deepest places within ourselves. We meditated long periods of time each day and slowly learned to listen within to the wisdom that comes from the heart. Our first child was born into this place of quiet and simplicity. We used her birth and presence in our lives to further our search for our center of love. She, of course, was a perfect teacher.

During this period of quiet, we were privileged to have Ram Dass (the Harvard professor turned spiritual seeker and teacher) move to our area. His voice was among the first to help start us out on a path of higher consciousness. We were blessed to enter a two-year period of in-depth counseling with him, and through his help, we were able to look at the darker side of our personalities and make a deeper peace with ourselves. There were few stones left unturned by the end of that period.

Many of our teachers helped us to understand the true nature of healing, that all healing comes from understanding the soul and from inner growth. Real healing takes place as we learn the lessons we came here to learn. Healing is an inner rather than outer process.

We also studied with a teacher named Pearl Dorris, who lived near Mt. Shasta, California, and who helped us to listen within before we spoke, wrote, or acted. She effortlessly conveyed her wisdom that all happiness, healing, peace, and spirituality come from within. Just by being herself, Pearl helped us to attune to our own inner place of knowing, our Higher Selves.

Although we were sincerely following a spiritual path, both individually and as a couple, Pearl used to laugh at how much we still operated from our heads. She teased us about it in the most delightful way. One day she decided to work with our mental, intellectual preoccupation. She led us through a guided visualization for entering the heart that we share now so others may benefit from her simple yet powerful technique.

ENTERING THE HEART

Close your eyes and imagine you are in a cluttered office: papers everywhere, piles of things to do. Now turn around and notice a door in the back of the office. Go ahead, approach it and open it. There is a staircase behind the door leading downward. Walk down the stairs. At the bottom of the stairs there is another door. Open it. Walk into a vast, light-filled room that is neither indoors nor outdoors. This is an expansive, sacred space like a beautiful temple or cathedral. It is filled with light and warmth, balance of color, uncluttered simplicity, and great beauty. You have just

traveled from your mind to your heart. Feast your senses
upon all that is here. . . .

Then she asked us to open our eyes. We felt a welling up of love
and gratitude for our lives and for each other. We were unmistakably
in our hearts. Since that time, it has been easier for us to distinguish
the difference between head and heart. Thank you, Pearl, for a profound lesson.

The greatest teacher of all was our love and the gradual connection we made to our original purpose in coming to Earth. We began
once again to feel the circle of light from which we came and the
instruction to live connected with this light and to help others do the
same. As soon as our connection to the light was strong within us, we
knew we could again try to work with a therapy group.

So in 1981, we again set up a group. This time it worked the way
we had envisioned. We were able to keep the "heart connection." We
had learned how to hold fast to each person's soul lessons and not get
lost in the psychological dramas. We were ready this time.

Our heart connection has been growing ever since. Our work
with people in workshops and counseling, in our writing and our
lives, is to listen within and feel the connection we all have to the
light. We feel this is how we help people the most. It is the simple
wisdom of the heart that gives power and purpose to all we do.
Ironically, the seven years in which seemingly nothing was happening in our careers proved to be the greatest training of all. For it was
through the inner listening that our work took on purpose and meaning. We can support others to the extent that we can listen within and
honor that place of wisdom within all of us.

Finally, we were beginning to live our purpose in coming to
Earth. The long and sometimes confusing preparation was well worth
the goal of connection to our Source. More, in fact, than our dedication to helping others with their relationships, we now strive to help
others make this connection to their own hearts. When they have
made this connection, they are living their purpose, for the two go
hand in hand.

Every one of us can learn to connect with our hearts, with our joy, with our life's purpose. It doesn't matter how long it takes to get there. As Lao Tzu said, "The journey of a thousand miles begins with the first step." What matters is that we take that first step, then another, and another. It is worth everything.

3

Light in
the Mirror

*On looking at what is in the mirror in front of you,
think of what is behind it.*

—Wu Wang

OYCE AND I SEE MANY PEOPLE WHO ARE STRUGGLING now more
than ever with their intimate relationships. For many people,
the pace of life is quickening and stress levels are intensifying.
At the same time, many people have grown painfully aware of
their lack of real connection with others.

Throughout our twenty years of practicing psychotherapy and
leading relationship workshops, we have had the opportunity to
study many couples over a long period of time. With many of these
couples, we have observed the initial high of falling in love. Over
time, some of them somehow deepen their love and the relationship
flourishes. Yet many other couples gradually lose their love and
enthusiasm for one another. Everyone wants to stay in love, but why
do some relationships make it, while others don't? Why does love
flourish in some relationships, but getting buried in others? What are
the secrets of a healthy and fulfilling relationship?

We've come to understand that in the relationships that make it, each individual is willing to make the relationship a priority, giving it time, energy, and nurturing. Each views the relationship as a beloved plant, which thrives with their care and attention.

Also, people in a prospering relationship are willing to look inside themselves, rather than only to their partner, for their growth and learning. They are willing to see their partner as a mirror—*a soul mirror*—reflecting back to them qualities which are within themselves, qualities they need continually to reclaim as their own. These partners are willing to trust this mirror of relationship. They are learning to take responsibility for their own lessons and issues, and they have learned that love itself is a reflecting pool. When their outer senses tell them it's "the other person's fault" in a difficult situation, they are willing to search deeper for their own issues that have contributed to the problem. Likewise, when their senses reveal to them the beauty, strength, and goodness of their lover, they are willing to search deeper for these same qualities in themselves.

The discovery that your lover is a soul mirror, reflecting back to you everything you need to learn about yourself in any given moment, will make the difference between a good relationship and a great relationship. This is acknowledging the mirror.

But there is another step in the process. It is seeing the *light* in the mirror. That means enjoying, rather than merely accepting or tolerating, the mirroring and viewing the process of mirroring with awe and reverence. *Accepting the soul mirror in your beloved will make for a great relationship. Loving and celebrating the soul mirror will create a sacred relationship, where there is no limit to the love that can be experienced.*

At the heart of this book are three beliefs that Joyce and I share: that love continually brings us back to ourselves, that each one of us is ultimately in relationship with ourselves, and this inner relationship *is* the spiritual path that most of us in Western culture are following. Our relationships with others can help us or hinder us, but the path we choose is our decision.

We human beings can easily get lost in our relationships with others. Relationships can become a seductive trap that pulls us away from ourselves, onto a long side-trip of life. Or they can be a power-ful vehicle that helps to awaken us to *who* we are and *why* we have been born. Our lives will not be fulfilled until we discover our own deepest purpose in life, which is to give and receive love, to enjoy the beauty of this world, to help create more beauty, and to remember that we each are an integral part of the whole. Each one of us is linked to all of creation. Each one of us is sustained by an omnipresent light, love, and consciousness. To be aware of this connection and give thanks for it is to live in the highest state of spiritual joy, peace, and fulfillment.

Inside and Outside

Every one of us has what it takes to bring more love into our life. It is our divine birthright. We deserve to love and be loved. To do so, however, we have to look two places—outside *and* inside. Our culture has trained us to look only outside, to look to others for validation and fulfillment, to see only the surface of ourselves and each other. We do need to look outside, to practice seeing beauty in others. Yet it is just as important to practice seeing beauty in ourselves, to know ourselves as beautiful, capable, and deserving of love. This takes will-ingness to look at ourselves differently, to see past the many limiting things people have told us about ourselves. In our souls, we are not bad, stupid, or ugly boys or girls. We are human *and* spiritual beings capable of the highest level of love and creativity.

Recently, rather than simply leaving a talking message on our office answering machine, I sang this song, written by Libby Roderick:

> *How could anyone ever tell you*
> *You were anything less than beautiful.*
> *How could anyone ever tell you*
> *You were less than whole.*
> *How could anyone fail to notice*
> *That your loving is a miracle.*
> *How deeply you're connected to my soul.*

It is our wish and prayer that each one of us discover our own inner beauty. In many ways, this is the highest work we can do to deepen all our relationships. When we give ourselves the time to feel who we are inside, in our souls rather than our personalities, we will see the purity, innocence, and lovability of a newborn baby. When we can see this in ourselves, we will see the same in others. In my own life, whenever I take the time to breathe peacefully and deeply, to quiet my restless mind, I can more easily remember who I really am. This will always help me in my life. A deeper view of myself gives me a deeper view of everyone else. I will then notice in Joyce aspects of her loveliness that I hadn't noticed before. I will see special qualities in our children that didn't seem to be there before. So loving myself allows me to love others. Seeing myself more clearly helps me to see others more clearly.

Just as the inner work of relationships—seeing into our own soul depths—is important, so is the outer work of seeing into the depths of others. When Joyce and I were in our twenties, we had a friend, named Lila, whose "hobby" was seeing the beauty in others. Her enthusiasm was contagious. We sometimes sat together appreciating one another (and whoever was with us) for hours. As we did this, we would rise together into higher and higher levels of joy.

Once, the three of us pulled into a gas station. While the gas tank was filling, I started to wash the windshield. I glanced inside the car. Joyce and Lila were talking, pointing at me and beaming. I knew at once what they were doing. It was a strange feeling to know they were loving and appreciating me, yet be unable to hear a single word. I started to feel self-conscious. I hadn't been feeling particularly loving. I had been in a very ordinary moment of washing glass. But my ordinariness was, to them at that moment, part of my beauty and loveliness. As I realized this, I could then feel what they were seeing, and a similar bright smile came onto my face.

Seeing beauty in another can be powerfully contagious. It helps the other person to see themselves as you see them. In this way, you become a mirror for them. Yet, they also become a mirror for you, for seeing goodness in another helps you discover this same goodness in yourself. You admire and appreciate someone's generosity, and in that moment you become more generous.

The beauty of relationships is that they point us in the direction of our soul lessons, the inner teachings we need to master. Being in relationship, especially in a close, committed relationship, offers fewer places to hide. So if we're trying to run away or hide from ourselves, relationship is a clear mirror in front of our face.

Our relationships with others offer us a mirror-like reflection of what is going on inside ourselves. Sometimes what we are attracted or repelled by are aspects of ourselves that we need to cultivate or deal with in a better way. So, depending on how we are feeling, qualities in others may or may not seem beautiful. For example, I was attracted to Joyce's easy expression of feeling. Why? Because I needed to develop this quality in myself. I thoroughly liked her expression of joy and love. Why? Because I was at peace with my own expression of joy and love. However, I didn't like her displays of anger. Again, why? Because I was not at peace with my own anger. Over the years, I have learned to see Joyce's emotional expressiveness as an admirable quality, no matter in what direction it becomes focused. As I have done that, my own emotional expression has been blossoming. That's because learning to appreciate a quality in another draws out that same quality in yourself.

The closer we become with another, the more we see ourselves reflected in each other's eyes. At a recent workshop, a couple stood up in front of the group to introduce each other. We were having people do this by describing in a few words what they most appreciated in one another. The woman smiled and described her partner as "love in my face." She then gave a look that told the group she had mixed feelings about this. Part of her was basking in the closeness of their love together. Another part of her wanted to run away from a mirror that was too close, reflecting her weaknesses as well as her strengths, her fear as well as her love, her pain as well as her joy.

The depth of our intimate relationships directly depends upon our acknowledgment of this mirroring. When we refuse to accept that our partner is holding a mirror up in front of us, we enter into unconscious projection, attributing to our partner what are really our own qualities. When Joyce appears unloving and I feel hurt, I can be quick to blame her. Often I have missed how unloving I was in that very same moment. It's easier to see the ways Joyce closes her heart to me, and harder to see how I close my heart to her.

On the other hand, sometimes I look at Joyce and see her as the most beautiful woman in the world (which she is!). If I ignore the fact that, through loving, I am looking into a mirror, then I am missing out on an experience of my own beauty. For the relationship to be fulfilled, we must be willing to look through the separateness of our partner toward a deeper recognition of ourselves. There is no doubt about it; this takes great courage.

Recognizing the mirror is important, because projection, unconsciously putting our inner qualities (whether good or bad) onto our partner, can be the destroyer of relationship. This process can be subtle and hidden from our awareness. Our counseling sessions and workshops are filled with people who insist their partner has a problem and they themselves do not. They remain stuck until they can acknowledge and look into the mirror on their partner's face and see how and what they are projecting onto them. This book is filled with examples of projection, and what it takes to break through to the light in the mirror and be spiritually fulfilled.

Until each of us takes full responsibility for all that is within us and stops pointing the finger at others, we cannot open to the fullness of love. We must see ourselves as the source of *all* our feelings, including all our reactions, rather than looking at what our partner did to "cause" our reaction. Seeing someone as causing our reaction is not taking responsibility for our own feelings. When we are willing to take this responsibility, our hearts can fly open. Our personal and spiritual growth depends upon our taking complete responsibility for our thoughts, our feelings, our actions, all that we are and all that we do.

Our relationships with others, therefore, are really secondary. They are background settings for the important lessons of the soul we need to learn as individuals. *When we make our relationship with our partner more important than our relationship with ourselves, we push away these very important lessons.* I have often tended to do this with Joyce. I am aware that one of my major life lessons is to nurture myself in the highest possible way. I do this by turning within, praying, meditating, breathing, and feeling the abundance of loving energy within and all around me. When being with Joyce becomes more important than being with Barry, I'm off base. Besides, I can't really be with Joyce until I'm with Barry. The deeper I am with Barry, the deeper I can be with Joyce.

THE PROMISE OF SOUL GROWTH

Every obstacle or problem that presents itself in relationship holds the promise of soul growth—*if* we are willing to look *inside* rather than to the relationship for the solution. The obvious reaction to difficulty or disharmony in a relationship is to want to get rid of it. But with a little patience and acceptance, we learn to discover a gift hiding behind every difficulty presented by our connection. In fact, the greater the challenge, the greater the gift.

For Joyce and me, the difference of our religious views threatened to end our relationship after only two years of knowing one another. We did go our separate ways, to schools in different cities. Yet this difference, and the pain we felt because of it, led us on inward journeys to discover the essence of Judaism and Christianity. We discovered that, in our deepest hearts, we believed the same truths, and this brought us closer than ever. This problem, this obstacle, led to soul growth, because we were willing to look inside ourselves, rather than outside, for the solution.

Here's another example of a gift arising out of a problem. A few years ago, Joyce and I became painfully aware of how much we were blaming each other. It was a stressful time in our lives, but nothing warrants blaming the other. The pain of that period, however, turned out to be a gift. One gift we received from this stressful time was our awareness of the unhealthy pattern of blame, a habit we started early in our relationship. Another gift was the determination to finally do something about it. We learned deeper ways of taking responsibility for our own feelings. If it hadn't been for this intensified state of suffering in our relationship, we might not have found the motivation to do something about a negative pattern that had been undermining our relationship for years. We share more about this in chapter 12, called "Anger in the Mirror."

When we reflect upon our relationship, every difficulty, every seeming barrier has blessed us with a gift. These experiences have given us more faith. We know there will be more tests, more challenges, but we trust there is a gift hiding behind each one.

This faith has allowed us to be even closer, to become even more vulnerable to one another. Early in our relationship, each serious argument threatened to separate us. With the awareness that we are mirrors for one another, together with the awareness of the gifts behind every challenge, getting rid of each other ceased to be an option. We realized if we didn't look into the mirror in front of us, we would have to find another mirror and start from where we left off. There was simply no place to run, no place to hide.

In those moments of pure projection, of strongly disliking each other, our faith in love's process would eventually shine through the mirror, and smiles would dawn on our faces. This is the grace of relationship; yet it is earned through diligent effort, awareness, and faith. The grace, the gift from Spirit, God, our Creator, love (or whatever name you use) is the privilege to share our heart with another. For a deep connection with another soul is one of life's most precious treasures.

Will any of our relationships ever be perfect? Not as long as we're living on this planet in these bodies. There will always be more to learn, discover, and master. But that's what makes the relationship journey so exciting. We're here on this planet to grow and learn as many lessons as we can.

I wouldn't trade these past thirty-four years with Joyce for anything in the world. There are moments when we are so much in love that we feel like a God and Goddess, surrounded and interpenetrated with the brilliant light of the cosmos. Sometimes during lovemaking, sometimes just sitting together, our hearts fill to overflowing with gratitude just for the privilege of being together in this life.

A few years ago at our Hawaii retreat, during our twenty-fifth wedding anniversary re-marriage ceremony, we stood looking into one another's eyes while Charley Thweatt and fifty people sang to us. We felt lifted above everything mundane by invisible arms of ecstatic love. We glimpsed more deeply than ever the gift we were giving to the planet just by loving one another. In awe of the sacred privilege of being together, we rededicated ourselves in service to the Light. We hope and pray all people everywhere can experience this—and more!

SEEING THE LIGHT IN THE MIRROR

Breathe deeply for a while to calm your mind.

Imagine you are sitting on a soft patch of grass in a beautiful garden. Warm breezes caress you with the sweet smell of flowers.

In front of you is a small pool with clear water and a bright, reflective surface. You lean over the pool to see the stunningly clear reflection of your face in the water.

Look deeply into your eyes, eyes you thought you knew so well but now seem to be discovering for the first time. There is so much more to you than you have ever known. Notice everything contained in your face. Notice the pain, the sadness, the grief from losses. Notice also the warmth, the happiness, the caring. All of this is there to be discovered in this clear reflection.

But now breathe more deeply. Notice a light that has always been present in this clear water ... a radiant brightness filling the water so full of luminosity that you are no longer sure whether you are looking into water or light itself.

Notice the glow in the reflection of your face, especially in your eyes. Your face looks like it could be twenty years old, yet it also appears ageless and timeless in its countenance of purity and deep peace. It is the most beautiful face you have ever seen.

Could this face still be you? Or is this another person you are gazing at? No, this is definitely you, but a deeper and more real you. The radiant light in this still pool is revealing your essential self.

Behold this reflection of the true you. Let your eyes drink deeply of your natural essence. Behold the light in the mirror! It is showing you a reality that you dimly remember from another time and place. But when or where is not important. Only here and now matters.

Look up from the pool. Someone you love is approaching from across the garden. This person sits on the grass beside you, warmly welcoming you to look into their eyes. These eyes appear radiant with love. It is effortless to look into them.

It feels like you have always known this face, these eyes, they are so familiar to you. As you gaze into the eyes of your friend, loving memories and experiences of times together fill your awareness. In this moment, the good and the beauty of your relationship outshine the struggles and the hard times.

Again breathe deeply and steady your gaze into these eyes. A familiar light is growing brighter, illuminating this person's whole face, revealing to you more and more beauty, wisdom, and profound peace. Yes, this is the same light that was in the pool, shining from and through your own reflection. Again, you're not sure if it's your friend's face you're seeing or your own. Your friend looks radiantly beautiful, shining like a sun, and yet it is clear that you are looking into a mirror. The face of your friend and the reflected face in the pool are just too similar.

You feel a welling up of love in your heart as you long to join, to merge, with this beloved who is you and who is not you. In this great love, it doesn't matter whether you are looking at your beloved or at a mirror of light reflecting your own heart. There is only one light, one radiant spiritual energy, shining in different ways, revealing different qualities.

Embrace this moment. Embrace the light in the mirror. Be at peace.

4

"Being" the Will of God

To see what few have seen, you must go where few have gone.

—THE BUDDHA

"HOW TO LIVE IN THE WORLD and Still be Happy" was the title of an evening in Santa Cruz benefiting the local Waldorf school. Barry and I were to begin the program, which featured Gayle and Hugh Prather, Jerry Jampolsky, Diane Cirincione, and Wally "Famous" Amos. Over 3,000 people packed the auditorium. Our talk was simple and direct, expressing our love and appreciation for children and family.

Now the talks were all over, and we were back onstage with the other speakers. It had been a meaningful and successful evening, and the applause was loud and joyful. The feeling onstage was one of victory and lightness. I felt carefree and childlike.

Suddenly, the clapping faded from my consciousness. I felt a light surrounding my being, and a sweet voice spoke to me from within: *You are pregnant with your fourth child. You are blessed and honored to carry this one.*

The light faded, the sound of clapping resumed. This could have been one of the most inspiring moments of my life. Instead, I fought against my wondrous news. At forty-two years of age, with two lovely girls on their way to independence and having had the experience of a baby dying in my womb, I did not want to be pregnant again. I felt like screaming, "NO!"

The clapping ended. People began hugging. Hugh came over and gave me a big hug. "That was a great talk you and Barry gave. I could really feel your love of children." He was quickly gone. I felt like a hypocrite.

Diane came over, embraced me, and warmly said, "I have read your books, and after tonight I can even more sense your love of family."

I was left standing alone again with my thoughts. How could this be happening to me? Again, all I wanted to do was scream, "NO!"

Barry came bouncing over to me, a boyish look of exuberance on his face. "We've been invited to the Prathers' for a party tonight. I know it's late, but let's go. It's been such a special evening."

"Barry, I'm suddenly feeling confused." I was struggling to find my voice. "Let's go home. I feel like I'm going to burst out crying."

He looked at me with concern. It was a big shift of energy for Barry, who was vibrating with excitement, but he said, "All right, let's go home." After all these years, he had grown used to a quality of unpredictability in our relationship.

On the drive home, I told him about my heavenly message and the news of a fourth pregnancy. Barry hopefully suggested I was pregnant with a new book or a new way of being. He kissed me, and I knew we could handle whatever came.

The next day, I found Barry in his office busily working on our upcoming schedule. He was excited as I entered the room and urged me to sit down beside him. He proudly showed me our plans for the next summer. He had arranged a weeklong international family retreat in the French Alps. Then we were doing a tour of Germany arranged by the German publishers of our books. The grand finale would be a two-week workshop and tour of Russia.

Barry's eyes shone as he spoke, "It has taken a lot of time and energy, but this will be our first really big international tour. Finally the girls are at the age where we can travel with them. We'll have a wonderful time!"

I looked at him with a pained expression and shared once again my revelation from the night before. Barry looked at me thoughtfully, "There is no way you could be pregnant. Your vision has to be about something else." We both understood that on a physical level there was an extremely small chance of me being pregnant.

"God works in mysterious ways," I reminded him.

"I know," he replied, "but how could a baby be coming when it is so clear to both of us that our work is just beginning to really reach out?"

I left the room wishing I had Barry's confidence that I was not pregnant. We both felt that God's will for us, a picture bigger than our intellects could grasp, was to reach out and touch more people. We had sheltered our two children at home for over twelve years. All four of us were now ready to expand, travel, and have new adventures. Another baby absolutely did not fit into this picture. With such "reasoning," I ignored the early physical signs of pregnancy, believing I had stomach flu. I helped Barry plan our upcoming summer tour, avoiding the intuition deep inside that we would do none of it.

Sometimes we don't understand the ways we are prepared for our next step in life. For us, this preparation came in the form of the death of our mother cat, Turn-Up, named because she seemed to only turn up for meals. She had given birth to four fluffy kittens. Ten days after they were born, she was killed in the middle of the night by a large roaming dog. We found the kittens in the morning and took them to our veterinarian, who told us they had little chance of surviving. He explained the many things we could do each day in an attempt to save the kittens. He concluded by telling us that even with the best of care, kittens of that age would have a tough time surviving without their mother.

We all felt that we owed it to Turn-Up to try our hardest. The four of us accepted the challenge, which proved to be more difficult than caring for a human infant. It took one hour to feed them all, and they had to be fed every three hours. Barry and I took on the night feedings. At first, the kittens grew weaker and weaker, then gradually they responded to our constant loving care. They began to grow and open their eyes. We all rejoiced at the miracle of their thriving.

One week after Turn-Up died, we needed to travel to Mt. Shasta to begin our river rafting workshop and Northwest tour. We were to be gone from the house for a month, so we had no choice but to take the kittens along. Our dilemma was to find someone we could trust to watch them during the six days we were to be on the river. Finally, a father and his ten-year-old son agreed to fill in for us for the six days. We knew it was a great inconvenience to the father, but out of his love for us he had readily agreed. Our family breathed a sigh of relief. We knew the kittens would be well taken care of.

Six days later, after the river trip was over, I knew for certain I was pregnant. The physical symptoms had become too strong to ignore. As I opened to this fourth pregnancy, I heard inside: *Remember how important it was for you to find the perfect situation for your little kittens? You did not mind inconveniencing the father and son, as you felt the kittens' care was so important. The father, out of his love for you and his gratitude for ways you have helped him, accepted the responsibility. This is a small example of what God, your Higher Self, is now asking of you. This precious soul, your fourth child, needs specific conditions for his earthly sojourn. He needs what your family has to offer in order to fulfill his purpose upon the Earth. We rejoice that he is with you. You will readily accept this gift out of your love for Spirit. The inconvenience you feel today is small compared to the blessing you will receive through mothering this soul.*

Two days later, a positive test confirmed the pregnancy. A baby was due in spring. Our family was in shock. Four healthy kittens played at our feet, reminding us of the miracle of life.

Through the experience of my fourth pregnancy, we have learned more about *being* the will of God, which is different from trying to *do* the will of God. We had spent much of our marriage trying to do the will of God. We tried to listen within and then act upon what we thought we heard. Yet, for the most part, we listened and acted upon what felt right and convenient in our lives. There was always the element of choice, which left us feeling content and in control.

Being the will of God, the source of all life, requires that we let go of our personal preferences, accepting in gratitude whatever is given, no matter how inconvenient it is to our lifestyle. *Being* the will of God is total surrender to a higher power and intelligence than our human mind can grasp in a finite moment. Another pregnancy was not our personal preference and definitely seemed to interfere with all forthcoming plans for our work. Yet our strongest desire was to serve God, to serve the light, and a fourth pregnancy was our next assignment.

Barry canceled the entire summer tour we had been so excited about and had worked so long to create. He canceled all travel plans for two years. We looked at other ways to earn our income. Providing for our family was going to be a real stretch. We began to think of expanding our already crowded two-bedroom home. Realizing there was no way, we just threw away a lot of nonessential stuff.

Each day, we surrendered more and changed our outer circumstances to accommodate this next assignment. Each day, our family sat together and meditated on God's desire for us. We tried to connect with God as our spiritual source, as the light within us. As we more and more became the will of God, our desire for the baby grew and grew. As our own plan began to merge with a higher plan for us, the inconvenience started to seem very small, just like the kittens. Through accepting the will of God and accepting our next assignment, all four of us were swept into a longing and love for our new baby.

As the months passed and I continued to throw away more and more possessions, I was amazed at how big a tiny two-bedroom house could seem. Barry refused all the fantastic travel invitations that came our way. The girls each prepared for what they would need to give up as a new baby entered their lives. All four of us discovered that we were being filled with a deeper peace through this process of substituting our personal desire for God's desire.

Spring arrived, and never had a family more excitedly awaited the birth of their little one. John-Nuriel was born on May 1, 1989, at 11:00 in the evening, outside and underwater in our hot tub. We were all in the hot tub in a little circle when his ten-pound body squeezed out into the water. We gently brought his face to the surface for air, while the rest of his body remained in the water. He was pale blue, somewhat limp, and was not breathing. We told him how much we wanted and needed him. He took a big breath and opened his eyes!

Oh, how much we wanted him! The canceled plans, the inconveniences, the lack of potential income, all seemed so trivial compared to the ecstasy of holding him in our arms. By stretching our lives to accommodate him, our hearts have been stretched and opened as well. His presence in our lives has blessed us each in a thousand ways. The "Nuriel" part of his name is Hebrew for "fire or light of God." We truly feel he has brought more fire and light into our lives and work. (A few years ago, I was sharing with a group of women how, before my first three pregnancies, the souls of Rami, Mira, and Anjel, our baby who returned to the heaven world, had knocked loudly on the door of my consciousness. Each one of them made it clear that they wanted to be conceived. Five-year-old John-Nuri was busily playing in the same room and, evidently, was listening to our conversation. He suddenly announced, "I didn't bother to knock. I knew you were too busy, so I just came!")

For all of us, God/Love/Light has a plan that is larger than our individual ego needs. Take a moment now to do the following practice, which will help you get in touch with that plan.

SEEKING YOUR NEXT ASSIGNMENT

For Couples

A wonderful practice for couples is to sit periodically, pray and meditate together, and ask God, the divine will, for an awareness of your next assignment in life. Ask without any personal preferences or limitations. Ask for what you now need to expand your relationship. How can you as a couple serve God in a fuller way? Whatever is given, accept it with gratitude, even if you do not at first understand. Trust that a higher power is guiding your way and giving you what you need step by step.

For Singles

Those of you who are single, and perhaps are seeking a partner, can ask in a similar way. What is your next assignment in life? What step can you take to come closer to being with your partner? How can you live your life so that you are serving more fully and growing in love? The answer you hear, or the circumstances life brings you, may seem like the farthest thing from your goal, but trust! Believe in a vision and intelligence higher than your own mind. Know that you are being guided step by step toward fuller happiness, harmony, and unity.

5

Two Magic Ingredients: Gratitude and Appreciation

There is always something beautiful to be found if you will look for it. This positive, loving attitude towards life and people is helping you to perceive the divine Presence, helping you to put into operation the divine magic which heals.

—WHITE EAGLE, IN
THE QUIET MIND

GRATITUDE AND APPRECIATION ARE TWO of the most powerful tools for soul growth in both relationship and in life in general. They are also perhaps the most simple— so simple that a small child can be taught to understand and master them. Yet these tools are able to change dramatically even the most inharmonious relationship. When practiced often, the tools of gratitude and appreciation can see a person through difficult times into a deeper and more fulfilling love. In our increasingly complex world, these tools may appear too simple and old-fashioned, yet it is their simplicity that allows them to be so timeless.

If we were told today that someone dear to us had only one more day to live, so much of what clutters our mind and life would fall away. We would then look deeply into the eyes of our beloved and tell them how much we appreciate them. We would hold back none of our love. We would see past all the barriers that keep us distant. It wouldn't matter whether they had an abusive childhood, were codependent, unspiritual, or overweight. We would have no excuse for withholding love. Our open-hearted appreciation and gratitude would be all that mattered.

We all have the capacity to feel the preciousness of each moment we spend with our beloved. We can remind ourselves that each day could potentially be the last chance to appreciate a loved one fully, to be grateful now rather than waiting for a time that may never come. I heard of a woman who lost both her husband and child in a car accident. She realized that living even one day without expressing gratitude and appreciation was a profound loss.

Another couple, Paul and Elizabeth, were right on the brink of divorce and decided as a last-ditch effort to practice gratitude and appreciation. They had a small child and wanted to do all they could. They sat together each evening, regardless of how they felt, and appreciated each other. They ended these sessions by thanking the other for their effort. At first, the appreciations tended to be superficial. Paul appreciated Elizabeth's good cooking or things he liked about her appearance. Elizabeth appreciated Paul's willingness to fix things that broke and the way he took care of the family financially. Even so, the couple sincerely sat together each evening and practiced anyway.

After several weeks, the appreciations deepened, the gratitude was fuller. Paul started seeing and appreciating Elizabeth's nurturing love for their child *and* for him. Elizabeth recognized and appreciated Paul's strength of commitment and devotion to her. After two months of this practice, the couple was well on their way to a new, more fulfilling relationship with each other. That was ten years ago. Their commitment has become a source of strength and a model for many other couples in their community. And they have continued their practice daily.

Our own family learned the importance of the practice of daily gratitude and appreciation in a dramatic way. We have always been closely bonded, yet even within that closeness we have had plenty of times of drifting apart. One of those times was when John-Nuriel was five months old.

Our family had been excited when our baby had been born. All four of us had pitched in with full enthusiasm for his care. Yet after five months, Barry, Rami, Mira, and I were growing weary. John-Nuri did not easily or gracefully adjust to his life on Earth. He cried and screamed just as much as he smiled and giggled. At age forty-three, I was a mature and seasoned mom, but I was not up to the rigors of this latest infancy. John-Nuriel weighed ten pounds at birth and was hungry from the start. He nursed almost constantly during the day and was up several times at night. I had a series of eight painful and resistant breast infections during the first two months.

In my fatigue and discouragement, I started neglecting my family's emotional needs. Barry had to take complete responsibility for our business and work, and became stressed with all the problems that emerged. Rami had turned thirteen and was beginning to act aloof from the family. Mira, our eight-year-old middle child, was having trouble getting attention from anyone. I yearned to be able to spend more time alone with her. An insidious distance was spreading among all of us.

Then something happened that shook us so violently that we have never returned to that place of uncaring, neglect, and distance.

Tuesday, October 17, 1989 dawned bright, sunny, and hot. The girls wore shorts to school. I kissed them as they went off, longing for more time with them. Barry went down to his home office, which was located in an already crowded laundry room. (We had an office in town, but he preferred working at home.) He seemed particularly absorbed in the difficulties of our business.

I was tending to John-Nuriel. Today he was full of smiles. He loved being all alone with me, content to nurse the hours away. I sang songs to him, read to him, and kissed his little hands. He nursed, so happy to be close to his mama.

As I nursed him, I looked around our little house. We had lived here for fourteen years. All three children were born here. All three books were written and published here. All five of us loved living here. The two-bedroom house was very small. About 15,000 of our books stored in the garage made it seem even smaller. Rami had the other half of the laundry room, which just fit her bed and little altar. It was separated from the rest of the laundry room by a curtain. Barry had cut out a window for her that looked out onto the bird feeder and garden. In her artistic way, she had made it into the most magical room of the house.

Barry's desk was squeezed opposite the washer and dryer. On the floor by his feet sat four bowls of kibble and water for our dog and the cats. He only complained when we piled laundry on his desk, spilled the animals' water so his feet got wet, or when I had to run the washer or dryer while he was on the phone. I often smiled to think of him in such a setting doing work that was so important to both of us.

The outside of the house was rather run down, an old red farmhouse that hadn't been painted in twenty years, revealing in many places the original white paint underneath. The faucets leaked, the front door didn't lock, and some windows couldn't be opened. We loved the house dearly. The rent was cheap, and we felt we could put up with the inconveniences.

The living room was large, and we kept it totally empty. We had all kinds of events here: workshops, Easter services, Christmas pageants, children's plays, weddings, baby blessings, and various other celebrations. Week after week, from twenty to eighty people crowded into our living room. Our home felt charged with the love and beauty of all who came to us. The healing quality of our work seemed to always pervade the atmosphere. Everyone who entered could feel the energy. Even the UPS driver commented on it.

The best part of the house was the land around it. One look out the dining room window revealed why we loved living here so much. A gorgeous 120-acre ranch spread below—a grassy valley surrounded by redwoods and oaks, with the Monterey Bay on the horizon. Except for an elderly couple down the hill who were the caretakers, we were the only people around. To say that we loved living there is perhaps an understatement—we adored it!

I looked down at little John-Nuriel, still nursing and gazing up at me with his gentle brown eyes. I was reminded of something disturbing—that during my pregnancy I'd had an unpleasant intuitive feeling that he might die before he was six months old. Whenever I would share this feeling with others, they got upset, saying I shouldn't project outwardly such a negative thought. It was a fear I therefore kept within. Our last baby had died when I was six months pregnant. Perhaps that was the cause of my fear. Before John-Nuriel was born, our favorite little six-month-old kitten, Mr. Sweet, was killed by a dog. As I held the kitten's dead little body, I felt a premonition that I might also be holding the dead body of my baby at six months old. Barry understood, perhaps because he shared a similar fear. Of course, we had no rational reason to support this feeling. We just had a sense that he might not live past six months of age.

John-Nuriel sat up from his nursing and gave a loud burp. He laughed. Burps always made him laugh. I hugged him tightly. He was a huge baby, weighing almost twenty pounds, strong and healthy. My love for him moved within me like the vast ocean.

"We've made it a long way, little guy," I told him as I tickled him. "Only thirteen more days to go," I thought to myself, remembering my feeling that he might die before he was six months old.

The day progressed as usual. I had an eye appointment, so in the afternoon Barry took the three children to the beach. It was so hot that they swam in the ocean, and several dolphins surprised them by joining in the fun.

I came home from my appointment early and had the house to myself. Normally, I would be ecstatic to have time alone. Not today. I worried about my family, eager to have them return. I felt a strange tension in my body, as if I was about to explode. The air felt hot and still, but that wasn't the problem. It was an eerie feeling. With each minute that ticked by, I felt worse. My only concern was to be with my family.

They returned at 4:30, exuberant and all talking at once about the dolphins. Even John-Nuriel seemed thrilled, pointing his fingers and jabbering away. Their mood of lightness and joy sharply contrasted mine. I was feeling worse by the minute. I laid John-Nuriel close to the bookcase, thinking I would make dinner. Perhaps being busy would ease the mounting tension within me. The massive bookcase stretched to the ceiling, holding six shelves of heavy books. This was one of John-Nuriel's "power spots." He loved lying there, looking up at all the colorful books. We used to laugh and say he was studying and absorbing their contents.

When I walked away from John-Nuriel toward the kitchen, the strange feeling within me increased to such intensity that I can honestly say I have never felt worse in my life. There seemed to be no reason for me to be feeling this way, but I did. I walked back to John-Nuriel and picked him up.

"Let's have a bath, fella," I said, deciding to postpone the dinner preparation. Baths were a favorite activity for John-Nuriel. As soon as I picked him up and moved him from below the bookcase, the tension within me eased to a tolerable point.

While John-Nuri and I were in the bath, Mira came to ask for help with homework. "Go ask Rami," was my reply at approximately 5:00 P.M. Rami was standing by the heavy door leading to the laundry room. She was reading directions for her own homework assignment. She looked at Mira, as her younger sister asked for help with her homework. Rami was all set to say "No" and continue standing there, when she felt a wave of love for Mira and walked the three steps up to the kitchen to help her, when. . . .

Shortly after 5:00 P.M., I went into the bathroom to help Joyce. I started the after-bath ritual by spreading a towel on the floor next to the bathtub. Joyce handed me our precious little dripping bundle and I laid him on the towel. At 5:04 P.M., as I was reaching for the corners of the towel to dry our baby, the house began rocking.

We have weathered many earthquakes. Nineteen years before, when I was a medical student in Los Angeles in 1970, we woke up early one morning as pictures fell off the walls, dishes crashed in the kitchen, and we heard a thunderous roar outside as a bridge collapsed a block away. We had just been initiated into our first major earthquake.

So, in those first few seconds in our Santa Cruz house, it felt much like the other rolling earth waves we had experienced. But this one got worse by the second! The house lurched violently. I could see by the trees outside our bathroom window that the house was moving. Built on the top side of a ridge, the house was clearly beginning to slide downhill.

Joyce screamed, "Barry, pick up the baby!" I tried, but the bouncing of the house threw me against the sink. I desperately tried again to reach for John-Nuriel, but this time was nearly thrown into the bathtub. Half the water in the tub poured over John-Nuriel, while he helplessly screamed and sputtered. The toilet crashed off its footing, and the broken pipe sent water splashing off the ceiling and walls. The noise was deafening.

Twenty seconds later, all was still. I quickly picked up a thoroughly soaked John-Nuri. With the power out, the pump stopped and so did the splashing. But the ordeal was not over. The gas line from our newly filled 250-gallon propane tank just outside the bathroom was sheared off. With a roaring whoosh, a thick white cloud of propane gas began pouring in through the open bathroom window, and our naked bodies were coated with propane. I grabbed our baby and turned toward the bathroom door, but debris from the cupboards and the cupboard doors themselves blocked our exit. I was aware that the tiniest spark could set off a blazing inferno. I handed John-Nuriel back to Joyce and fought my way through the clutter.

Finally the door opened and we made our way over the crazily uneven floor to the living room. There we met up with Rami and Mira, their faces white with fright. They had been in the kitchen, amidst the worst mess in the whole house. Rami's legs were bleeding from half a dozen cuts from flying pieces of glass. Blood was dripping from Mira's head, where she'd been hit by a falling plate. The entire contents of the kitchen cupboard had emptied over them.

Our family reunited, we made our way over fireplace rubble in the living room and through thick clouds of dust that were still settling. I noticed that the floor and ceiling were separated from the walls, but it wasn't until we got to the front door that we realized the full extent of damage to the house. It was then I knew with shocking certainty that we would never live in this house again. We had to jump across a chasm to our concrete porch. From there we could see that the house was five feet off the crumbled foundation, totally destroyed. By the grace of God, the roof had not caved in upon us all.

We helped each other out to the dirt road to view what had once been our home. The house and almost everything in it at that moment appeared totally destroyed. Rami started screaming. John-Nuriel was still coughing and choking on the bathtub water. Eight-year-old Mira cried and asked, "Are we going to the heaven world now?" And I imagine that to a child, it could have easily looked like the end of the world. . . .

Barry suddenly threw up his hands in ecstasy, shouting, *"We're alive! We're alive!"* We stood in a circle, thanking God and shouting, *"We're alive!"* We kept hugging each other with the deepest sense of appreciation. In that moment, as we stood naked on our road, not knowing if we could recover anything of our material world, we were made aware of what is most important in life. Our home and possessions had been taken from us in twenty seconds, but we had each other. Standing among ruins, we found we had gratitude and appreciation for the most important things of all—our lives and one another.

As we stood there, naked and holding each other, we heard the sound of a motorcycle roaring up our hill. Approaching us was a tough-looking man dressed in black. He pulled right up to us and stopped. It would have made a very interesting photograph, this rough-looking person with slicked back hair and a large black beard asking caringly if we needed his help. We thanked him and sent him down the hill to check on the elderly caretakers of the ranch, who also lived in an old and poorly built house.

Barry turned off the gas and checked the girls' cuts. When we saw that the house was not about to cave in, we ventured back inside.

Once there, we realized how close we had all come to either serious injury or death. John-Nuriel's "power spot" by the bookcase was a huge pile of fallen books and shelf boards. We shuddered at what might have happened if I had left him in that spot when the earthquake hit.

The door Rami had been standing near, before she went up to help Mira with her homework, had sprung off its hinges and shot across the laundry room and out the window. Rami would have been in the path of that door had she remained standing there.

The kitchen floor was covered with broken glass and dishes, appliances, and spilled food. There was nothing in any of the cupboards or on the counters. Had the earthquake lasted even a few seconds more, the house would probably have slid down the hill. The roof was close to collapsing in several places.

It is an absolute miracle that all five of us survived the earthquake with only minor cuts and bruises. It is a miracle that we are alive to tell about the experience. We are convinced the angels were working overtime.

The silent distance that had been creeping into our family vanished, leaving in its place gratitude and appreciation for one another's presence. We now cannot look at each other without realizing how close we came to dying and how precious our time together is. The fatigue, discouragement, moodiness, and acting out that had begun to separate us now seems trivial and unimportant. All that matters to each one of us is the gratitude that each is alive. After the earthquake, we could not say enough how much we appreciated each other.

It was twenty-four hours before news from Santa Cruz reached beyond our city. Friends and relatives were frantic. When I was finally able to reach my parents in Buffalo, New York, my mother told me that many people had figured out how to contact them on our behalf from information in our books. Her voice choked with emotion as she told me how much love was being poured out to our family. She said, "Your dad and I and Barry's parents have often wondered why a medical doctor and nurse would choose work with so little financial reward. But today I understand where your wealth is. It is in the gratitude and appreciation of all these many people you have worked with. You have chosen the greatest of wealth."

And it's true. The greatest investment we ever made was to share our hearts fully with others. Now we needed to draw upon that investment. We decided to follow through with a planned weekend couples retreat starting Friday evening, three days after the earthquake. Ten of the twenty couples still wanted to come. We brought our children and allowed everyone to bathe us in love. The girls were having difficulty sleeping at night because of dreams of the earthquake.

We gave everything we had at that retreat, but more than ever before, we *received*. At one point on Sunday morning, I was not able to hold back the tears, and Barry asked everyone to hold us. John Astin sang, *"Blessings on your journey ... on your way back home ... just carry the light within you."* As the tears flowed, we once again realized that "Home is just a feeling." We felt how much help is available to us at all times. We felt the presence of the angels and the illumined ones who have never stopped helping and guiding us. We felt how much everyone was willing to help us—and we needed a lot of help. We were so grateful for the outpouring of love from our beloved sisters and brothers. In that moment, we gazed into one another's eyes and rededicated ourselves to doing God's work—the work of continually opening our hearts to giving—*and receiving from others.*

Although we were aware of the hand of God in this disaster, we still had the human feelings of grief, loss, and sadness. With each aftershock, we relived the earthquake. Sometimes it seemed like a bad dream from which we would soon awake. This was especially true when we returned to the house, a little part of us hoping to find it intact. More than once, we wistfully thought of the miniature aliens in the movie *Batteries Not Included,* who miraculously fixed anything that was broken.

Gratitude and appreciation were the tools that saw us through a year of tremendous change, stress, and difficulty. When the feelings of grief, loss, and sadness threatened to overwhelm our family, we remembered that we still had one another, and gave thanks to the Light.

Shedding Our Costumes

A few days after the earthquake, we moved into a house that none of us liked. A friend told us it was the only available house in the county, so we rented it. It was cold and dark, surrounded by asphalt, near a busy road, and far away from everything familiar. After putting up with this for six months, we decided to try an experiment and camp for six months with our two daughters and baby son. A neighbor next to our destroyed home offered his beautiful undeveloped property to us. On April 8, we moved the possessions that weren't destroyed by the earthquake into storage. With camper and tents, we set up "house." Returning to the land we loved was both healing and painful. We watched with nostalgia as a bulldozer tore down the house in which the children had all been born, but we felt happy and fulfilled just being together.

At first, the experience was enjoyable in its simplicity. April and May are lovely months in the Santa Cruz mountains. The rains usually stop in April, and we have sunny, clear skies while enjoying cool ocean breezes. It rarely rains in May, my favorite month of the year, with orange poppies and blue lupine everywhere. When I decided upon the camping experience, I imagined the usual ideal weather.

On May 14, it started to rain. Everyone celebrated, glad to extend the greenness of spring—except me! The rain continued for two weeks. Have you ever tried camping in the rain with two children and an active baby boy? After the first week, I started to fall apart.

We were invited to dinner at the home of some wonderful friends. When we arrived, they warmly greeted us and our big bag of laundry. The woman ran to put our clothes in the washing machine. While it was washing, she asked me, "How are you coping without a home? How can you stand it? You must be worn out from having to work and take care of children without a home base." I was silent, aware only of a deep ache welling inside me.

She continued to put words to my own doubting inner voice. "The children must be having a hard time without a room of their own. How can Rami study?" The ache inside me was growing. I glanced down the hall at four exquisite little rooms, one for each of their children. My lovely friend of ten years was drawing out a deep pain within me, a pain that I had refused to acknowledge for over a week.

That night, I cried deeply as the rain continued to pour down. Our beds were damp. Our clothes were damp. And my mood was very damp. Barry held me close. A camper at heart, he tried to point out the positive side of our experience. It didn't help. I felt I couldn't take another day, I wanted a home so badly.

The next day, it again poured rain. Barry and the girls left for work and school. I stayed in the damp camper with John-Nuriel, trying to think of someone to visit so he could crawl and play. The ache inside me was almost overwhelming.

Later that day, as our baby slept, I sat and prayed for help. How could I find happiness in this situation? I waited. I went outside in the wet and cold. I sat and waited and prayed. Then I remembered that my soul desired only to love, serve, and remember God. I knew this was all I truly needed, but little by little I had begun to take on a "costume" of things I thought I needed to wear in order to be happy and complete. One of the parts of my costume was a physical home. Somewhere along the road of life, I had gotten the idea that I couldn't be happy without a home. Another part of my costume, as a parent, was that I thought I needed to provide a cozy room for each child, and there we were, all thrown together in one damp, uncomfortable space. Through visiting my friend, I felt the inadequacy of my costume. How could I be happy without a full costume to wear?

As I prayed, I saw that a costume was just an external form that could be changed or even taken off whenever I wished. I realized I could find happiness right now by simply shedding my desire for these intricate costumes. I could be happy here and now, right in my present situation. I realized that this opportunity of homelessness was giving me a chance to simplify my costume, to shed a layer of what I felt I needed to be happy.

I reflected on the many costumes people wear. Some people feel they can't be happy without a mate or without children. Some feel they can't be happy unless they have exactly the right job situation. Or perhaps they think their costume is incomplete if they do not act a certain way, earn a certain amount of money, or have a certain appearance. It goes on and on. . . .

I began to see that the only way to change my circumstances was to be truly grateful for the situation just the way it was. As I began to feel grateful for the camping experience, the sun suddenly burst upon our campsite for the first time in two weeks. Rather than focusing on the damp boxes of children's clothes, I saw the flowers that Rami and Mira had planted in old pots for me on Mother's Day. The flowers had thrived in the rain and were glowing with color, flowers planted with so much love by children who love their mother. I looked past the muddy, sponge-like rug Barry had rolled on the ground for the baby to crawl on and remembered how close we all felt to each other. The closeness of our living situation had brought out more closeness in our relationship.

As I became more and more grateful for my situation, I saw more and more beauty. As I gratefully shed parts of my costume, I felt light and free. I danced around our campsite, thankful for the mud, dampness, cold, and wet—thankful also for the growth these situations caused in my soul. Just as seeds need moisture and light to grow, the wetness of my tears mixed with the sunlight of gratitude was bringing new life and beauty into my being. I felt once again my true home and original "costume" of life: to love, serve, and remember God. Our original costume can shine in any situation and in any relationship. Gratitude and appreciation are the keys to unlocking the sunshine.

EVEN MORE BLESSINGS

Joyce and I have experienced many gifts and blessings from the Loma Prieta earthquake. It has helped us to understand more deeply the divine workings behind the scenes of all seeming adversity.

In geology, as the years of built-up pressure between the Earth's continental plates is suddenly released, the region becomes more stable. True, the pressure may again slowly build over the next twenty to thirty years, or it may not. No one knows for sure. After a major earthquake, however, there is a new stability, a new beginning, a fresh chance.

The same holds true in our relationships. The pressure of our unhealthy habit patterns (such as dishonesty, projection, blame, judgment, and criticism) can build until they explode out of us, usually at whomever is nearest. The explosion (like the earthquake) can hurt both the other person and ourselves, but can also clear the air and open the way for real growth. The phoenix rising from the ashes, spreading its wings to soar up out of darkness and destruction, is a resurrection metaphor. The message is simple: Something good is eventually born out of darkness, disaster, or seeming evil. We just need to look a little deeper to see the light shining from inside.

For us it was a brand-new house. Next to the little red house that was destroyed by the earthquake, there was a sixteen-acre piece of land. There was a magical trail that ran the length of the property, with a gorgeous view south across a wooded valley with Monterey Bay in the distance. We felt so at home on this land, even more at home than in our rented house. Every day, we walked the magical trail, finding power spots for meditation. Not once did we ever see anyone else hiking there. The land began to feel like ours, and we took care of it accordingly.

Since 1974, during a meditation retreat in the French Alps, Joyce and I nourished the vision of a place where people could leave their busy environments to come into an atmosphere of love, acceptance, and healing. There, they could discover their own inner wisdom, either in a loving supportive group or alone in nature. Before our home was destroyed, we dreamed of someday owning the sixteen acres ourselves.

We found out the property was an investment for a wealthy lawyer who lived a few hours north, near San Francisco, and had only seen it once—the day he bought it. Every few years, we sent him what we felt was a fair offer based on current market value. Each time, he wrote back asking for approximately twice what we'd offered. This went on every few years for most of the fourteen years we lived in the old house. Our offers went higher and higher. His counters kept doubling our offers. Finally we gave up making offers, but we could not give up our feeling that this was sacred land. We continued to care for the property and meditate in special places.

On the morning of the earthquake, I started out for my usual walk onto "our" trail, surprised to see a woman coming toward me from the property. She said she was a realtor, and then announced that the property was in escrow. Someone was buying "our" land. I can still remember the sick feeling in the pit of my stomach as I returned to our house and sat down. This just couldn't be happening. I carried a feeling of depression (and not-rightness) the whole day. The earthquake happened later that afternoon.

Months later, while in the rented house we did not like, our thoughts and feelings returned to the sixteen acres. We were reminded again of our vision for it. For all we knew, someone had bought it and was by now planning to build. We called the old owner anyway and were told it was still on the market. He seemed friendlier. We learned that shortly after the earthquake, unknown to us, the new buyer had come up our hill. He saw our destroyed house, must have panicked, and promptly dropped out of escrow. He hadn't known how poorly our house was built, with a totally inadequate foundation.

After the earthquake, a lot of people were leaving Santa Cruz County. Homes and land were flooding the real estate market. Prices were plummeting. The owner agreed with us on a price for "our" property that turned out to be much lower than our offer of several years before. This was yet another important lesson on how loss often turns into gain. After hearing our story, people teasingly blame us for causing the earthquake so we could afford to buy this land.

We are now living on the sixteen acres, in a home that has been built to withstand a much greater earthquake than the one in 1989. We call it the "HomeCenter," because it is equally a home and a center for our workshops and retreats. The large living room/meeting room is built directly over the spot where we meditated and wrote our previous books. It has always been a power spot for us. Now it is a power spot for many people.

We often give thanks for the heavenly wisdom that has guided us every step of our journey. The earthquake has given us even more faith in this divine help. We will always remember the earthquake as a powerful teacher of two magic and essential ingredients of life and relationship—*gratitude and appreciation.*

GRATITUDE AND APPRECIATION

Gratitude and appreciation can open the door of your heart to any person or situation in your life.

For a Loved One
For one week, focus your gratitude and appreciation upon someone close to you. Pay attention to all the little, and usually unnoticed, things as well as the big things this person does for you. Whenever you can, thank them for something they have done, no matter how small.

At the end of one week, take some time alone to deepen the practice. Inwardly, appreciate the soul qualities of your loved one. Feel your gratitude for the blessing of being with this person. Pray that you not take this blessing for granted.

For a Situation
As we practice feeling gratitude for all the situations in our life, we will find ourselves letting go of the past, being less concerned about the future, and dwelling more and more in the eternal present moment of the open heart.

In your quiet time, feel grateful for all the situations that have brought happiness into your life. With each situation, allow your heart to open ever wider.

Now, reflect upon one situation that is hard to be grateful for. Look for a way this situation has come into your life to teach you a valuable lesson and bring a gift of growth. As you can embrace this situation with gratitude and appreciation, the gift and the growth will be more fully present in your life. If you cannot be grateful for this now, give thanks that in time you will find the gifts.

6

The Power of Appreciation and Constructive Criticism

Happiness is the art of making a bouquet of those flowers within reach.

—GODDARD

PPRECIATION OF THOSE YOU LOVE—whether a lover, a parent, a child, or a friend—is one of the cornerstones of living a spiritual life. Verbally pointing out beauty and strength in someone you love is a way of bringing more depth to a solid relationship, healing to a wounded relationship, or renewal to a tired or stifled relationship.

Barry and I often begin a talk or workshop with an appreciation exercise. We understand people may feel appreciation for one another. Still, we like to give them more opportunity to show it. For a relationship to work, there needs to be much more appreciation than criticism. If the balance is more on the side of criticism, the relationship will go steadily downhill, leading to resentment, anger, and distance.

Appreciation is a fuel that continually feeds the flame of love.

So how do we appreciate? True appreciation comes from seeing and acknowledging the inner being rather than the outer personality of the person we want to appreciate. This is also the basis of forgiveness. We can easily become fixed on a person's seemingly harmful or unconscious actions and respond by closing our heart. Yet, if we look a little deeper, behind the actions, we will see another child of God just like ourselves reflected in the light of our partner's eyes. We will see a beautiful soul sharing with us the same journey to the light. As we seek to uncover the divinity within ourselves and others, the quality of our relationships will rise to limitless heights.

Daily appreciation can work miracles for a relationship in trouble. Taking time to be positive with your partner can change a destructive energy pattern into a constructive one.

Sexuality, in particular, is an area of relationship that longs for appreciation. I cringe whenever I hear someone running down his or her partner's sexual performance:

"He doesn't know how to touch me in a satisfying way."

"She's like an iceberg in bed."

"My other lovers never had his problem."

Comments such as these, said in the presence of a partner, are extremely harmful. Sexuality is an especially sensitive area of relationship. If a partner is judged negatively or compared unsatisfactorily to a previous lover, it can cause a deep wound of insecurity. This wound can fester and grow, causing serious problems.

A better way to approach sexuality, especially when there are problems, is through the healing power of appreciation. Each partner needs to feel their efforts to please and satisfy the other are noticed and appreciated. If you feel your partner needs to make changes in a certain area, you help them most by appreciating what they are doing right—and saying this often. Then, with great sensitivity to proper timing, communicate what needs to be different. In the middle of an argument or late at night when you are exhausted is usually not the best time to do this.

If your partner attempts to make changes, appreciate their every effort. Sex is an act of love, not a performance. If you keep your heart tuned to the love your partner is expressing, rather than the performance, and appreciate the uniqueness of that expression of love, you will more fully enjoy the experience.

In a women's group I was leading, I once asked a woman who had been happily married for forty years to tell us her secret. Without hesitation she said, "Every day, I tell my husband how much his lips turn me on. And every day, he responds with a broad smile and passionate kiss." Besides making us all laugh, this woman's advice is very good. Our partner wants to know we are attracted to them. Every partner wants to feel they are a beautiful lover. It is our appreciation that brings this feeling. When our lover feels appreciated, it helps him or her feel more confident. And more confidence helps them try all the more to give love and affection.

Appreciation is also important in parenting. Children need to be reminded often about their beauty. If children do not receive enough appreciation, they will begin to lose their sense of their inner beauty. Children are open and vulnerable. When they are criticized, they accept and internalize the negative comments said to them. Children who aren't appreciated enough learn to become adults who don't know how to appreciate.

Appreciation can help heal wounds that develop between parent and child. If a child or teenager senses that you believe in them and see their beauty, they will be much more cooperative and loving toward you. When you as a parent feel you cannot even talk with your teenager without fighting, you can visit their room when they are sleeping at night. Even the most rebellious teenager still looks like a sweet child in sleep. As you gaze at your teenager, allow your heart to be filled with the appreciation and love you feel for them. If you feel sure they will not wake, you can whisper your words of appreciation. Parents have reported an almost miraculous change once they started doing this. Their teenager, even though asleep, absorbs the appreciation and love.

CONSTRUCTIVE AND DESTRUCTIVE CRITICISM

On the other side of appreciation is criticism. Sometimes we need to confront our lover with something they do that makes us feel uncomfortable, but this is a tricky and delicate business. Criticism given with love and sensitivity can bring needed changes. Without these ingredients, criticism can wound a relationship and alienate two people from one another.

Perhaps the greatest rule for using criticism in a relationship is to make sure your words of appreciation far outnumber your critical ones. We have found that the expression of appreciation is a far greater and safer tool than criticism. If there is an abundant flow of positive comments and love, then a necessary criticism once in a while will be more deeply heard and can motivate growth. Human beings respond much better to love and appreciation. Believing in the beauty of another can bring about the deepest growth and most positive change.

Sometimes it is tempting to share a criticism about someone we love with someone outside the relationship. We suggest that the first rule about criticizing another is to *do so directly*. Gossiping about your lover is a sure way to undermine your relationship.

When Barry and I were first married, in many ways we were both still bonded to our own parents. We made a rule that no matter how difficult our relationship became or how much we at times disliked each other, we would never say a negative word about one another to any of our parents. It was so tempting in our early marital conflicts to ask Mom or Dad to side with us against our "awful" partner. We never did this, and thus gave our parents a free, unencumbered chance to love our partner.

We gradually extended our "rule" to include everyone outside of our marriage. No matter what criticism we have of each other, we will not speak it to others. Criticism of each other stays privately between us and is worked out within the relationship. The only exception to this is when we have gone for help or counseling, and we know the therapist or advisor will not take sides. This practice of not gossiping has served us well in our relationship. It has been a powerful force for good in both of our lives as well as building a deep trust. It has kept us focused on the sacredness of our relationship. We try to extend this practice to all we are in relationship with: our children, our parents, and our friends.

Sometimes it is difficult to differentiate between constructive and destructive criticism. Barry and I once had a teacher and counselor we went to for help in our relationship as well as our individual lives. At the time, we felt stuck in certain ways of being and relating and didn't know how to change. Sometimes our counselor criticized us harshly, but there would always be a twinkle in his eye or a smile playing about his mouth that revealed his great love and compassion for us. He believed in us and he believed in our relationship. Sometimes he said awful things to hear—like pointing out how attached we were to a certain thought or feeling—and his smile would turn into a chuckle. Soon we were smiling ourselves, and quite often we began laughing at our own foolishness. The whole time he was criticizing our behaviors, he was loving *us* and honoring the deepest qualities of our souls. A criticism from him actually felt good to receive and inspired us. These were examples of constructive criticism.

One day, I went alone to see him and I could tell he had been having a hard time in his own life. The smile and twinkle were gone that day from his face. At the end of our time together, he sharply criticized my relationship with Barry, saying he doubted we could make it together as a couple. I felt hurt. When I got home, I cried and felt confused. The criticism from this man in the past had inspired me to make some big changes in my life. He had held up a powerful mirror and lovingly encouraged me to break out of old stuck patterns of living, to grow and become all I could. The recent words hurt my heart. I felt betrayed, sad, and powerless. Barry held me for a long time while I cried. He kept saying over and over to me, "Is it possible that his words were a projection of his own inner hurt and confusion?"

I pondered this for a long time, then realized this latest criticism didn't have the familiar ring of truth for me. It had depressed and wounded me. I had not felt this person's love while he spoke. This was destructive criticism. Even though I dearly loved this man, I could not accept all he said to me as truth for my life. My guide for knowing the truth of a criticism was the inspiration it brought to me.

I wrote this man a letter expressing my feelings. Some time later, he called and apologized to me. My letter helped him to realize something. He told me he had been going through a difficult time in a relationship and had felt threatened by the closeness between Barry and me.

If a criticism is true for our life, we will feel an inner inspiration and rightness about it, no matter how hard it is to hear at the time. When we have to criticize another, it is important that we try to hold the beauty and essence of this person in our awareness, so they feel *our love* as well as our criticism. If the person we are criticizing becomes defensive, perhaps we have not been as clear and loving as we had hoped. Try again later, using even more appreciation and respect.

A final rule for constructive criticism: *Share how you feel rather than delivering blame messages.* Making the other person "wrong" creates more separation and distance between you. Sharing your feelings, which were perhaps triggered by the other person's actions or words, invites that person into your world, to see you better and to understand their impact upon you. This can lead to a dialogue that can bring more love and closeness.

THE "SHELVES" OF APPRECIATION

Expressions of appreciation and love do not always come in the form we would choose. We can cling to our ideas of how we want love to be shown to us, or we can accept and acknowledge the ways we are already appreciated. We are constantly being given gifts of love, but because of how they are presented, these gifts often go unrecognized, or even worse, we reject them. How often do we fail to accept gifts of genuine love because they do not come in the form we want? To deepen ourselves and our relationships, we need to be alert to the gifts of appreciation that come our way, each in their own unique package, and feel the love behind each act even if it doesn't come in the form we'd like.

Barry and I got married when we were twenty-two. I moved from my parents' home in Buffalo to join Barry in Nashville, Tennessee, where he was a first-year medical student. This was the farthest we had ever lived from our parents. We rented a small apartment and furnished it from second-hand stores. I worked long hours reupholstering chairs, painting tables, and fixing up our home. It was my first time as a homemaker, and I wanted our place to be just perfect.

I looked forward to my parents' first visit, wanting so much for them to be proud of me. In fact, I was cleaning right up to the moment they knocked on the door. It was an important time for me, the first time I could welcome my parents into my own home.

My mother walked in first and was full of compliments for all the ways I had fixed up the apartment with so little money. My dad walked in behind her carrying some pieces of lumber and his tool box. He was silent and started inspecting all the closets. I began to feel hurt. He wasn't saying anything positive.

The next morning at 6:00, I was awakened by the sound of sawing. I jumped out of bed and ran to my dad.

"What are you doing?" I asked, annoyed.

"You need a shelf here in this closet," he mumbled, barely looking up from his work.

I looked at the mess of sawdust and pieces of old lumber on the floor and lost my patience with my dad. I wanted him to be proud of me for my first home, and here he was making a mess. "I don't want a shelf!" I said as I stomped out of the room.

He continued to put up the shelf. We never spoke about it. After he left, I found myself ignoring the shelf my dad had just built. It remained empty the entire time we lived there.

Two years later, we moved to Los Angeles, where Barry would be finishing medical school. I set up my second apartment. My parents again came for a visit, this time by plane. I noticed one of my dad's suitcases seemed very heavy. "I brought my tools, just in case," he casually remarked. My mom was again full of compliments about the apartment. My dad was silent. This time, three shelves went up. I didn't get upset, but I also didn't particularly care about the shelves.

Several moves later, we settled in a home in Santa Cruz, where we lived for fourteen years. My parents visited every year, and every year, more shelves were added to the home. As our first two children grew, my parents stayed and cared for them while we led our Hawaii retreat each January. It became a ritual to return home after the retreat and look for the new shelves. My dad would never point them out to us. He always sat in the rocking chair buried behind his newspaper, acting as if he didn't even know we were there looking at all his new work. Each year, many new shelves would be built. Toward the end, he was running out of room for new shelves so he started building little shelves within the older shelves.

My dad and I don't sit and talk about feelings the way I wish we could. He likes to talk about the news or repair jobs on his home. When I was younger, I felt hurt that he seldom appreciated me with words and never could tell me he loved me. Over the years, I have grown to accept the reality that these shelves are my dad's way of saying, "I love you, I care about you, and I am concerned about you." He is uncomfortable translating those feelings into words. He feels embarrassed. The shelves *were* his way of saying, "I love you."

I began to appreciate the difference between a person's words and their actions. Some people are better with words; others are better with works. Some can say beautiful, loving words but are inconsistent or lazy in their actions. Others can make a powerful statement without any words at all.

The home that probably held more than a hundred of my father's shelves was totally destroyed by the 1989 earthquake. The shelves are all gone. My dad is eighty-two years old and has slowed down considerably. Now he talks about where he thinks Barry should put shelves. The physical gift of the shelves is gone, but the legacy of love carried by them remains forever within my heart, my dad's way of saying, "I love you!"

Perhaps someone in your life is presenting you with a gift you are not recognizing as their way of expressing love. As you can acknowledge this gift and feel the intention of love behind it, you can open to an outpouring of love that will bless your life. Look for those "shelves" and receive them deeply into your heart.

Following are appreciation practices for both individuals and couples. Joyce and I believe these practices have benefited all our relationships, especially our own partnership.

OFFERING APPRECIATION

For Individuals

Close your eyes. Breathe deeply to relax your body. Breathe into and out of every part of your body—not just your lungs.

When you feel settled down, bring in front of you a relationship you wish to heal or enhance. Visualize this person sitting before you. Remember a special time of closeness with this person, an experience you shared that allowed you to see this person's soul more clearly. Perhaps it was in the beginning of your relationship, perhaps later on. Try especially to remember the feelings of closeness you shared. What qualities about this person endeared you to them the most? What was it about this person that attracted you to them? Take enough time to feel these things.

Now, realize these same qualities are present just as strongly as ever. It's just that you have let them drift from your view. Look more deeply at this person's image in front of you. Notice these beautiful qualities coming to the surface once again, almost as if the image was previously out of focus and now you can see more clearly. This is a remarkable being in front of you, filled with power, beauty, and love. See and feel this for as long as you can.

As you can see this in your visualization and feel this in your feelings, you will more easily see and feel the same beauty with your outer eyes and senses. Let this inner practice give you the courage to now give one of the highest gifts we ever give in our relationships. Find a time to share your appreciation with words. Create a receptive atmosphere for your partner or with whomever you focused on in the practice, and let this person know what you most appreciate about them. Give this as a gift to them, to you, and to the relationship.

For Couples

Sit facing one another with your eyes closed. As with the first practice, quiet your mind through breathing deeply or through any other method you prefer.

When you are ready, open your eyes and look silently into your partner's eyes. Look past your partner's face and personality through their eyes—the windows of the soul. What is it about this being in front of you that touches your heart most? What qualities attracted you to this soul in the first place and allowed you to rise in love? What gifts are you receiving from this friend? How is your life being blessed by this relationship? Let these questions put you in touch with your deepest feelings of love and appreciation.

Whichever one of you is ready to begin can now put these thoughts and feelings into words. Let the words flow from you unrehearsed and spontaneous. Be courageous in your vulnerability. Let your "inner poet" speak without inhibition. Practice expressing thoughts and feelings about your partner that you have never expressed before. Take turns speaking and watch the doors of your heart fling open.

Practice both the inner and the outer exercises as often as possible. Together, in a balanced way, they will bless and enrich your relationships.

7

The Perfect Partner

We are not two, yet you look for me outside; when you find me within yourself, your own naked mind, that single awareness will fill all worlds.

—YESHE TSOGYEL

FROM THE TIME OUR WORKSHOP BEGAN, Elsie, a woman in her late sixties who had been divorced for a number of years, was longing to know how to find a mate. She wasn't looking for just anyone. She felt she was now ready for her soul mate, her life partner, her kindred spirit. And she wanted to know where he was.

Sunday after lunch, partly with Elsie in mind, I did something Joyce and I sometimes do in workshops. I spread a deck of the *Shared Heart Cards*, containing our favorite quotes from our first three books, face down on the floor. I told the group to inwardly ask for what they needed in their relationships with their loved ones, and then pick a card. I watched as Elsie picked her card, looked at it, and then grimaced. I asked her to read her card to the group. She instead announced that she wanted to put her card back and pick another. It was clear to me from the expression on Elsie's face that she indeed

had the perfect card. I again asked her to read it. With much reluc-
tance, this is what she read: "The true soulmate is a state of consciousness . . . not a person."

People sometimes have difficulty with that statement from *The
Shared Heart*. It is a great temptation to look outside of ourselves for
the answers we need, but our soul mate, our highest spiritual partner,
can never be found outside us, no matter how hard we look. For it is
not someone separate from ourselves. The challenge is to take
responsibility for being our own soul mate, and that requires loving
ourselves in the way we wish someone else would love us. It often
seems much more convenient to have someone else be our soul mate
so we don't have to look deeply inside of ourselves.

How many times, especially in our earlier years, have I foolishly
tried to change Joyce so she could better fit my ideal of the perfect
partner? I wanted her body and face to look different, more like a col-
lage of images from years of watching TV and movies. I wanted her
to walk and move more gracefully instead of having a childlike
bounce in her gait. I wanted her to wear different clothes, to be more
reasonable and even-tempered, and less emotional. The list went on
and on. . . .

Joyce, similarly, wished she could change me. Often we seemed
to pounce on each other, mallet and chisel in hand, determined to
create the perfect partner. As Joyce described earlier, we finally softened in this determination to change the other, realized how much
we loved one another, and decided to get married. But we hadn't completely given up the hope of molding one another, even through our
love, into a more perfect partner.

I remember after much difficulty finding a person willing to
marry us (our religious difference in the early '60s was still a big obstacle), we finally came across a minister who said he would marry us on
one condition—*that we promise to honor the differences between us!* When he
put that condition upon our wedding, we knew he was the right person to marry us. And we knew this was the right commitment to make
to one another.

Over the years, Joyce and I have been learning to accept one another as we are—complete with differences, personality quirks, flaws, and beauty. Trying to change each other is refusing to accept our partner as a soul mirror, reflecting aspects of ourselves which we need to see *if* we want to learn more about ourselves. Trying to change our partner is, thus, a refusal to grow spiritually ourselves.

We have seen so much sorrow in people's quest for the perfect spiritual partner. We have also seen profound soul growth. Andrew and Julie, two friends of ours, had what we felt to be a "life partner" relationship. We saw the issues they were working on, and we knew they had what it took to work through them. Their love was strong, as was their commitment to their hearts and to one another. So we were all shocked when Julie suddenly ran off with another man, claiming she had found her true soul mate. Andrew was devastated. He sank into despondency, at one point even thinking about suicide.

A few months later, Andrew was beginning to pull his life together when he met a woman with whom he fell in love. We saw him soon after that. He looked like he was floating on a bubble that could pop at any instant. There was a pie-in-the-sky smile on his face. He wasn't all there, but what could we do? We weren't about to point out to him the fragility of his condition. You just don't do that to someone who feels they are in love, especially when they are not asking for your feedback. We wished him well in his new relationship, and let him be.

It took six more months for the bubble to burst. Andrew's girlfriend left him to be in another relationship. Again, there was the shock, the sinking into despair, the loss of hope, the grieving. We comforted him as much as we could.

About a month later, we bumped into him at another friend's house. He was beaming. Somewhat cautiously, I asked him how he was doing. He told me he was engaged to be married. I looked closer at him. There was something different about him. He seemed more grounded, more peaceful, more rooted in himself. He smiled at me, turned his head to one side, and showed me his newly pierced ear adorned with a lovely earring.

"This is my engagement present," he announced with a smile. "I created a ceremony and got engaged to myself. I'm planning a very special wedding ceremony. It'll just be me, making vows to love myself, all alone at my favorite place in nature."

I was so happy I embraced him. He had finally learned the "soul mate lesson." He learned that his true soul mate could never be found in another person. He was about to wed his inner soul mate. By doing so, he would be able to enter relationships with others from a place of more wholeness.

We can all benefit from Andrew's story. How delightful it would be if each of us created such a ceremony for ourselves. Why not? Who does not need to love themselves consciously more and look less for fulfillment from outside?

Some esoteric spiritual traditions speak about the "mystical marriage" as the joining together of the male and female aspects of oneself. They describe each soul as being androgynous, equally masculine and feminine, but losing this balance in the process of growing up in a male or female body. Part of the process of the spiritual quest is the rejoining of the inner woman with the inner man, the reintegration of the two inner polarities. This rejoining into wholeness is the most sacred of weddings that a spiritual initiate passes through.

We touch upon the mystical marriage when we embrace what we love in a partner as being a part of us. We move toward integration when we accept that our beloved is really a mirror, reflecting back to us all the qualities of our inner partner. Seeing beauty in Joyce is a way of seeing the beauty of my feminine side, but I need to take responsibility for the beauty I see as being a part of me, not just outside me. In this way, every conscious relationship can help each one of us with our own inner "mystical marriage."

When our inner man weds our inner woman, we become whole, integrated, and fulfilled human beings. Then our relationships with others will reflect this same wholeness. We then dance with our partners as equals, rather than with a feeling of incompleteness. How much greater the joy of the dance! How much deeper the love!

THE "UNSPIRITUAL" PARTNER

Some people feel stuck with a partner who they feel is far from the "perfect spiritual partner." Here's a letter we once received from a woman: "I feel frustrated! While I look for new ways to grow and fulfill my creative desires, my husband seems content to sleep, eat, go to work and watch ball games on TV. If I want to truly grow, do I need to leave the marriage?"

If you feel you could also have written us this letter, you first need to decide whether to stay in this relationship or not. This may not be obvious, for you will only know the answer in moments when your heart is open, when you feel your love for your partner. In your frustration, in your resentment, or even in your tolerance, you will not be capable of seeing who your lover really is and what your relationship is all about.

It is important to take some reflective time by yourself, every day if possible. In these times, try to penetrate the ball-game-watching ("unspiritual") exterior of your partner and see this person as someone who, like yourself, longs for growth and fulfillment, for that is certainly there within everyone. If you can do this, it will eventually become clear whether you need to stay or leave.

Just as important, realize the "unspiritual" exterior of your beloved is a mirror, reflecting back to you the unspiritual side of your own personality. For your own growth, it is imperative that you confront and accept the hard-to-accept parts of yourself. Have you closely looked at your own laziness? How about the judgmental part of you that sees your beloved in such limited ways? Accepting this mirror will also help you to see the relationship more clearly—with its beauty, with the work *you* can do on it, and with the potential for growth it is providing you.

If your decision is to stay in the relationship, and if you really do "look for new ways to grow and fulfill your creative desires," you have a creative challenge ahead of you. You have the opportunity to draw out the latent beauty and power in your partner. Your challenge is to discover that inner part of this person. Before you can have a positive influence on your relationship, it is important to re-vision it, to see it in a deeper way. And you do this by seeing your mate in a deeper way—and communicating it.

Did you ever consider that your partner isn't so fulfilled watching his ball games or living life in a mechanical way? Did you know he loves to love, but perhaps forgets he does? Did you know you have unlimited possibilities to creatively love him and draw out his love? Have you forgotten how much you need his love—how wonderful it feels to be loved by him, not just sexually but really LOVED? Did you know that if you *really* gave him an opportunity to show his love, he'd be willing? Did you know that giving him an opportunity to love is giving yourself love?

Be as creative as you can. Your effort is for you just as much as for your mate. When you can see his goodness and beauty, he will be reflecting back your own goodness and beauty. Most importantly, don't neglect time alone, time to visualize the deeper parts of your beloved, yourself, and your relationship. It's like building a house and spending too much time on the construction site. You need to frequently refer back to the "blueprint" to remember just what it is you're building.

Ultimately, it never works to judge another's spiritual development by their outer pursuits. Remember, *we are human beings, not human doings.* More than how much a person meditates each day, are they kind to others? Do they feel a basic respect and consideration for life? Do they appreciate nature? Are they willing to give of themselves to someone in need? These are more accurate measures of a person's spirituality.

THE "SPIRIT PARTNER"

A woman once asked us in a letter if it was possible to have a "spirit partner." She wrote, "I have often felt like I was missing someone I've never met, and have yet to find the relationship that I dream about. Since no relationship has ever come close to my dream, I've never gotten involved. Anything less than a relationship with the perfect soul mate seems too casual, and my ethics now won't tolerate casual relationships."

This feeling (or way of thinking) can help as well as hurt our spiritual growth. It can help by keeping us focused on the highest vision of relationship, the heavenly gift in the union of two hearts. Many of us can relate to the loss of interest in "casual" relationships. Although Joyce and I have been in a deeply committed, spiritual relationship since 1964, there are still times when our relationship becomes too "casual" or superficial. At those times, we have to remember who we are together and bring the needed depth back into our relating.

The down side of holding out for the perfect spiritual partner is that she or he may never show up. The truth is, there is no perfect partner—that is, perfect according to our own thoughts and desires. And even though we may understand this concept, we still have to contend with the longing in our hearts to share this journey of life here on Earth. We each have a deep need to learn powerful life lessons, a learning that the process of relationship accelerates. We need a relationship with another person's body and personality and feelings and thoughts—the whole far-from-perfect package, not his or her "spirit" alone.

To hold back because we haven't met "the one" is to postpone the possibility of tremendous growth. We know an abundance of single people who judge relationship "prospects" much too critically: This one's body is not quite right. That one's smile is not straight enough. He's a little too much "in his head."

One man told us he seemed to have a knack for picking "wounded" women to rescue. Then, when he realized her "wounds" were beyond what he felt capable of helping, he felt compelled to end the relationship. I pointed out that he was just as wounded as they were. This was the reason he attracted these women to him. The problem was not their wounds, but his neglect of his own. He was unconsciously projecting his inner flaws onto these women. This is another example of what happens when someone doesn't pay careful attention to the mirror aspect of relationship.

Comparing everyone you meet with your mind's image of the perfect partner will guarantee you isolation from intimate relationships. No one will ever compare favorably. Really, the ideal image you are seeking is your own higher self, your inner light body which you are always (if sometimes very dimly) aware of. It is tempting to project this divine self outward, to want to meet this one through another. Yet, unless you first accept this perfect divine partner within yourself, you will not recognize the higher self in another.

On the other hand, it doesn't work to jump into relationship with anyone who comes along, just because you know the perfect partner doesn't exist outside of yourself. You can open your heart to everyone who comes along, in the sense that you are willing to give and receive the highest love that you can. This is very different from becoming sexually intimate with everyone in the name of loving them. This latter is a manifestation of relationship addiction, the seeking of a relationship "fix" outside instead of inside, wanting to be loved *by someone else.*

Sometimes I look at Joyce and remember the teenage list of qualities my perfect partner needed to have. My list has changed over the years. As I have been embracing my inner soul mate, I less and less need Joyce to be that for me. Consequently, I more and more see the beauty and perfection of Joyce's qualities. I love the way she looks, the way she walks, the clothes she wears. I appreciate how different she is from me, giving me opportunities to stretch past the limits I've placed upon myself. I love how she accepts me, letting me be exactly who I am. We're far from perfect, but we're learning about unconditional love. We're seeking the soul mate within and letting one another be.

How do you recognize the potential for a true spiritual partner? You need to listen to your heart for the prompting to go deeper with any given person. This prompting is a feeling that may be very subtle and is felt differently by each of us. It may come quickly and then be followed by the rationalizations and judgments of your mind. For some persons, these inner promptings may be totally obscured so there is only confusion about whether to go deeper with someone. So what do you do? You learn by trial and error. You learn by doing the things that stretch you beyond your limits. If it is easy for you to push away from people and be alone, you experiment with more closeness. If you are with someone because you are afraid they will feel rejected if you leave, you experiment with leaving as consciously as possible. And if you are afraid of becoming too close to someone because they might not turn out to be the "right one," far better to have given your all and endured the pain of not having the relationship last than to have withheld your love out of fear. Knowing that the perfect partner is *within you* will give you the strength and courage that you need.

Many people go from one relationship to another, seeking, searching for the mirage of the ideal mate. The challenge of life is always to seek that special friend within, to learn how to fall in love with love itself, to seek first the "kingdom of heaven" within us. Then there will be peace, and in that peace there will be the knowing of what to do, or with whom to spend this lifetime. When we have finally made friends with ourselves, there won't be that urgency to find some perfect partner outside. We will have the patience to allow for the wonderful timing of the universe. We will be unfailingly guided toward someone of true soul compatibility, someone with whom we can share the path of love and service to the planet.

SELF-LOVING

For this practice, you will need to either sit holding a hand mirror or stand in front of a wall mirror.

Close your eyes and take some deep breaths. Now make eye contact with yourself in the mirror.

Before you can love another person, you need to love yourself. Said another way, the amount you love yourself is the amount you can love another. It's so easy to think relationship is only about loving someone else. This is natural. It's what we have been taught all our lives. But all relationship starts inside—with loving ourselves.

Go ahead, look deeply. You are a beautiful, divine, radiant being! You are so much more than you normally see in the mirror. Look at yourself the same way you would look at a beloved friend. Love yourself in a way you wish someone else would love you. Don't get stuck looking at your hair, your makeup, the circles under your eyes, or your newest wrinkle. Look deeper. Look at the light in the mirror, the glow of love that shines through your physical face, the you that is beneath the surface. Is there a commitment or vow of love you would like to make to yourself at this moment? Doing this will help you in all your relationships with others.

8

The Doubting Mind

Our whole business in life is to restore to health the eye of the heart whereby God may be seen.

—SAINT AUGUSTINE

KNOWING THAT WE ARE EACH WITH THE RIGHT partner gives Barry and me a deep sense of joy. Eliminating doubts about our relationship from our minds has allowed for more creative use of our energy. Doubt consumes a tremendous amount of mental and emotional energy, especially when it concerns such an important part of our life—our primary relationship. Knowing in our minds and hearts that we are in the right relationship enhances every aspect of our lives.

Every year, Barry and I meet hundreds of couples from all over the country. Occasionally we meet two people who have been together for a long time and still love each other very much. Whenever we meet such a couple, we enthusiastically interview them. Without exception, the couple will credit the success of their relationship to a strong commitment and willingness of both partners to go through the hard times together. These couples invariably share that they have had major turmoil and pain in their relationship at least one time over the years they have been together. Each one states that when they stood committed, it allowed them to go through the hard time with each other. Even though it was a painful time, they did not doubt their connection to each other. They have all reported feeling even more love and respect for each other, having gone through something difficult together.

Now, are these couples just very blessed to be with the perfect partner, or have they each trained their minds to overcome doubt and fear about their relationship? I feel that the latter is probably true. There is no such thing as a perfect partner, one who will always give you unconditional love, demand nothing, never push your buttons to make you upset, always be sensitive and understanding to your every need, has the wisdom of a sage combined with the lightness and enthusiasm of a child, has a body that is always attractive in appearance, and is always ready for sex whenever you want it. This type of partner simply does not exist. The perfect partner is a fantasy of the mind seeking inner perfection. The truth is that our partner will sometimes be all that we want them to be and other times will be unable to focus on our needs.

Our souls are constantly seeking perfection, wanting to dwell in harmony with the divine. Some of us are more aware of this than others. As we become more aware of our inner need for harmony, we have less need to demand perfection from others. We can judge less and accept more.

If you have ever given birth as a mother or been at the birth of your child as a father, you know the feeling of unconditional love. When you see your infant for the first time, you feel a deep sense of commitment and love in your heart for your child. Holding your newborn for the first time, you feel you will never abandon this being. You helped bring them to Earth, and you will stay by their side for as long as you are needed. Parents usually think their newborn is the most perfect child alive.

But just as there are no perfect partners, there are also no perfect children. As these perfect babies grow, they begin to oppose and bump heads with their parents. Most parents accept this behavior from time to time, and few doubt (at least for long) that they have the right child or that they made a big mistake by helping to bring this soul to the world. Most parents will try their hardest to keep their hearts open to their children and not give up on them. That is why a separation may happen between a parent and a child, but seldom a divorce. Most parents train their minds to be committed to their children.

This same experience of unconditional commitment can be applied to all our relationships. We hope that when two people get engaged or married, they feel a sense of commitment toward each other as well as a deep love and respect. There is a spark of love and joy that makes them desire to step forward in deeper union with one another.

What causes that commitment, love, and respect to turn sour, causing a couple to seek separation and divorce? The mind takes over the feelings of the heart and begins to doubt the experience. The mind sees something it doesn't like or experiences hurt or pain, and it begins to doubt whether the relationship is right. Maybe it would be easier with someone else, we think. These thoughts of the mind, if left unchecked, can sabotage even the deepest love and respect. The shortest marriage we have known was just three days in duration. How quickly the mind took over the initial experience of the heart.

The feelings that accompany doubt are sadness, fear, anger, and depression. Often a person will feel sadness concerning the relationship and wonder why. They are not aware of the doubt in their mind that was the forerunner to the sadness.

We need to look deeper. Where does this doubt come from?

We all have a human tendency to doubt the good that comes into our lives, to feel unworthy or undeserving. This is the deepest and most basic level of doubt. Of this doubt we are more or less conscious. We then unconsciously project this self-doubt onto our significant relationships, making these other persons appear less than satisfying or not worthy to be in relationship with us. This is another way that relationship becomes a looking glass. To doubt the worthiness of our partner is to in some way justify the doubt we feel about our own worthiness. It is only a ploy that keeps us from looking at ourselves.

So what do we do with doubt? The trick is not to give all our power or attention to our doubting mind. When a thought of doubt about the relationship arises, notice it, but then bring the mind back to the inspiration of the heart that brought us to this person. Remember, and try to feel, the original experience of love and attraction you had when you were first together. When we come back into the experience of the heart, the energy that caused the doubt is usually not present.

An example of doubt in my life came shortly after our daughter Mira was born. My guidance to conceive her was clear and effortless. She came to me as an unborn soul, spoke to my heart and told me she was ready to come. I knew I was blessed to be able to be her mother. The pregnancy and birth with her was easy and beautiful. I was totally in love with her. The first three weeks of her life were quite blissful. Then Mira began having a hard time. She cried almost continually for several weeks.

One morning, I got out of bed after a particularly agonizing and sleepless night with her. The thought went through my mind, "Maybe I made a mistake by having Mira. Maybe I don't want this relationship." Just two sentences of doubt, then my mind went on to more immediate concerns. I was unusually sad all that day. Even Mira's playful smiles could not cheer me up. The doubt of the early morning was long forgotten as I concentrated on caring for Mira and five-year-old Rami. Mira had a great day and slept for a long period, allowing me a chance to rest and play with Rami. Rest and time with Rami usually brought much joy into my life. Not that day! I felt filled with sadness.

Barry offered to watch both girls when he returned from work, and I sat alone in a place where I prayed and meditated. I closed my eyes and tears flowed down my cheeks. I prayed and asked to be shown the source of the sadness I was experiencing. Presently, the brief thoughts of doubt about Mira returned. The power of these thoughts, having come twelve hours previously, had affected me all day. I realized that these doubting thoughts had nothing to do with Mira and how much I loved her. They came from a place of self-doubt. *Her crying was making me feel inadequate as a mother.* Her crying was mirroring my own inner crying.

With this realization, I thanked God for the gift of Mira in my life. I let my heart feel how deeply I loved her. I let myself feel and accept that I was a good mother. As I felt my willingness to go through all the hard times with her, my joy returned.

My hard times with Mira did not stop with that prayer and realization. She still cried and fussed for several more weeks, and we had many more sleepless nights. My attitude, however, did change. I stopped doubting the relationship with her. When thoughts of doubt would arise in my mind, I would notice them and then allow myself to feel my original inspiration in having Mira. I would also feel all the ways that I am a good mother. Noticing these doubting thoughts and bringing my mind back to the inspiration of motherhood gave me the energy and vitality I needed. This practice has helped me in all my relationships.

Relationships need care every day to ward off feelings of doubt. What if someone gave you a beautiful garden of magic flowers and healing herbs, and told you that this garden would be a constant source of growth, love, and deep fulfillment for you? The only thing you needed to do to keep the garden alive was to water and fertilize it regularly and pick out each weed before it grew too big. If you really knew how wonderful and special this garden was and that it would bring you an abundance of gifts, you would carefully weed and nurture it as often as possible.

Our relationship is this garden. The weeds are the thoughts of doubt. The water is the love and nurturing you give to each other. Relationships need to be watered and weeded every day. If done with care, your garden of relationship will become ever more beautiful with each year. Your harvest will be love, joy, laughter, and a deep sense of well-being as you help each other to fulfill your purpose.

There are times when one or both of you change in such a way that the doubt you feel about your relationship becomes very great. Early in our marriage, Barry announced to me that he needed to be free to be intimate with other women, and ended up having an affair. This was a major change. In the three years that we had been married up to that decision, we had had a monogamous relationship. I had a very serious doubt that I could stay in the relationship. I knew I had to say "No" to Barry to honor my own feelings. Had he continued in his need for sexual connection outside of our relationship, our marriage would have ended.

How does a couple know when a doubt is serious or is just one of the many little doubts that come in the course of a relationship? The knowing comes through careful observation and a willingness to weed out all of the little doubts before they become big. Barry and I had always given our relationship the top priority in our lives. We weeded the garden of our love every day and showered it with attention and nurturing. Even though we were young, untrained, and had the time-consuming commitment of medical and graduate school, we somehow knew the importance of weeding and watering on a daily basis. When this particular weed appeared in our garden, I knew it was different from the others. There was no question that this weed tested our relationship, and if allowed to stay would cause our garden of marriage to die. It was my choice to say "No" to this weed, but it was Barry's choice to pluck it out or allow it to stay in his garden. Fortunately, Barry plucked the weed, but because it was so big, it caused damage to the garden that took several years to restore. Once restored, our garden became more beautiful than ever.

There are major weeds that can creep into a garden of relationship: drug and alcohol abuse, infidelity, and physical violence are some of the biggest invaders. Sometimes these weeds cannot be plucked out easily, and the garden withers away. The couple senses a need to separate. Their garden is no longer bringing them beauty. Most weeds of doubt begin small and can be discovered soon enough to pluck them carefully out. If this is done often enough, the garden of your love and friendship will flourish, bringing you a lifetime of beauty.

As you enter into a relationship or if you are in a relationship already, commit yourselves to weeding out the little thoughts of doubt as soon as they arise— and differentiate these little doubts from the more serious ones that require strong action.

For the nagging doubts that aren't relationship-threatening, train your mind to replace these doubting thoughts with ones of gratitude and appreciation. Train your mind to observe the mirror in front of your partner to catch projections. Gently remove these bothersome weeds from your garden. You will find that this practice will bring much beauty to your relationship and to your personal life. Tenderly water your garden of love with nurturing appreciation and affection. You may discover that you are with the right gardener. This knowing will bring a peace and power to every phase of your life. Your energy can then soar together to new heights of divine love and relationship. People will be blessed by the fragrance and abundance of your garden. Some will receive a flower and will treasure its beauty for a lifetime. Others will receive sustenance which will nurture their own gardens of relationship. The radiance of your garden will be a source of inspiration for many. All this with a little tender weeding and watering!

WORKING WITH DOUBT

Every good gardener knows the importance of plucking out the weeds as they come. If the garden becomes taken over with weeds, it loses its beauty, and the task of eliminating the unwanted intruders becomes more difficult.

As a thought of doubt about our partner comes, replace it with a thought of love and appreciation. If the same thought comes over and over, look at it carefully to see if you are ignoring the mirror and projecting your own negativity onto your partner.

If you still feel this doubt and cannot transform it through positive thoughts or through introspection, then share this thought of doubt with your partner. Angry or stressful times are not the right moments to share this thought. Share it in a space of respect, and healing and understanding can come.

9

Overcoming Our Fears of Relationship

The two of you are a reflection of each other, the One God masquerading as two bodies, two minds, two hearts, perfectly complementary to each other.

—JOYCE AND BARRY VISSELL,
IN *THE SHARED HEART*

WE HAVE MET MANY PEOPLE FOR WHOM hardly anything can be more frightening than being in a deeply committed relationship. Many fear losing themselves or their power in a close relationship, or they are terrified at the prospect of becoming vulnerable only to be painfully abandoned by their beloved. The irony of relationship, however, is that it doesn't have to take us away from ourselves at all. Relationship can be a mirror, offering us a continual opportunity to find ourselves. Indeed, that we find ourselves by looking into this mirror makes relationship a magical, wonderful, and transforming experience.

The challenge, however, comes when the mirror reveals to us not just our lovability, our beauty and strength, but also the shadowy places within ourselves. So the deeper, more primordial fear in relationship is not our fear of anyone or anything outside of ourselves—it is our fear of what is inside ourselves. Facing the inner demons that appear in the mirror as we draw closer to another can be our greatest spiritual hurdle. Yet, with such confrontation comes knowledge, a sense of triumph, and a greater ability to love ourselves and others. As we bring the scary shadows of our own souls, or psyches, into the light of our conscious love and acceptance, they become less scary, and we grow in spiritual strength and compassion. This chapter will focus on some of these fears, their origin and how to work with them, as well as the risks individuals and couples can take to overcome these fears.

THE FEAR OF NOT BEING WORTHY

Perhaps our greatest fear is that we are not worthy of love, that we don't deserve to be in a healthy relationship with someone who loves us unconditionally. We are afraid that we are unlovable because of the mistakes we have made in the past, because of the negative things people have told us about ourselves, or because of the painful ways we have been treated. Too often, we link our sense of self-worth to how successfully we fulfill roles in life. We associate who we are with our actions, rather than seeing ourselves as the miraculous, light-filled beings that we are. As we grow in awareness of who we *really* are, our self-love grows, and so do our relationships. As we love ourselves more, we attract to us people of like awareness, people who love themselves more.

THE FEAR OF LOSING YOURSELF

Many people fear losing themselves or their power in an intimate relationship. This fear has caused some to stay out of close relationships altogether and others to keep a certain amount of emotional distance from their partners.

First, it is important for us to take responsibility for our own sense of power. No one can ever take our power from us or cause us to lose ourselves. It does no good to blame another person. We alone allow such loss. We lose our power or feel ourselves becoming lost when we make another person more important than ourselves—when their voice and desires become louder, more insistent, and more important than our own inner voice. There is a delicate balance that must be maintained between listening to our partner and listening to the voice within our own heart. Within each of us is the God Presence, the light within our heart—our own inner guidance which is helping us to grow and become the truly magnificent beings we are meant to be. Our most important task in life is to listen to this inner voice or feeling. When we fail to listen inwardly, when we make our partner's voice more important, we begin to feel lost or feel our power draining away. Our true power comes from making contact with our Source, the God Presence within. Our partner's voice can never fulfill that need within us. Knowing this at the outset is essential to create a growing, committed relationship.

Each day, then, we have the wonderful challenge of balancing between listening within as well as listening to our partner. As we consciously practice this balancing with our partner, we will enter into a state of true communion. Our inner voice will begin to resonate with the inner voice of our beloved. Both of us will feel recharged, as we will have tapped into our source of power simultaneously, affirming and strengthening one another. This is one of the most beautiful qualities of relationship, when two people can help each other listen to their own inner voices and communicate that inspiration to the other. Taking the time to listen within, to claim our God-given power and beauty, and then to hold to the truth that we feel, is one of the greatest gifts we can give to our partner—and to ourselves.

RECLAIMING YOUR POWER

Take some time alone, preferably in a natural setting.

Now ponder these questions: Do you feel there is a way you have given up your power in a relationship? Have you let a partner's voice become more important than your own inner sense of rightness? Is it happening now?

In this time of solitude, claim your inner power and beauty. Affirm, "I am just as wise and important as my partner. My inner light and strength are a gift to my partner and to the world."

Sometimes a relationship involves taking a big risk. When you were growing up, did you ever visit a swimming hole in a river on a hot summer's day? Perhaps there was a rock or a high bank from which you could jump into the water. Perhaps you had not seen anyone ever jump from that spot and you had not done it yourself yet. Naturally, you might slip into the water and feel carefully for shallow areas, branches, or rocks. Then, assured of safety, you might try the jump.

It is not quite the same with relationships. Sometimes we have to dive in head first without any guarantees of safety. We may not even know how to swim. Yet jump we sometimes must. We're not saying we have to act impulsively or foolishly. There first must be a kind of inner "go ahead" letting us know that despite fear or doubt we need to take the leap anyway.

In 1968, after being in a relationship with Joyce for four years, I was afraid of losing my freedom and my power through marriage and commitment. The voice of my heart, however, kept saying, "This is it! She's the one! Jump!" Another part of me was terrified!

Joyce was in the middle of her final year at Columbia Nursing School in New York City. She felt she needed a commitment from me. I told her I didn't feel ready to get married; wasn't it OK to just keep things the way they were? No, she said, not for her. She wasn't willing to keep sitting on the fence, so she submitted an application to the Indian Health Service to work on a reservation in New Mexico after graduation. She told me of her decision not as a threat but as a way of letting me know she needed to move ahead with her life. Perhaps some part of me interpreted her action as a way to pressure me into commitment. I don't think I believed she would go through with it.

Sometime later, Joyce informed me that she was accepted by the Indian Health Service. Still I remained in stubborn denial. Then she bought her plane tickets (in those days they were refundable). I started to rouse from my denial. Could it be that Joyce would really leave me to work on an Indian reservation? It started to sink in that she not only could, but she intended to. And she was not doing so to pressure me in any way!

I now had some inner decision-making work to do. I took the time to think and feel seriously about my relationship with Joyce— something I might not have done had Joyce not taken action for herself and begun to pull away. I started to examine whether making a commitment to one person by getting married was in fact losing my freedom, losing my power, losing myself! The truth gradually dawned on me. I once again glimpsed the vision of our relationship together. By the two of us loving one another and joining in the deepest way, the love generated by that joining would be greater—*we* would be greater—than the mere sum of our two hearts standing alone. By joining fully with Joyce, I knew I would be gaining (rather than losing) love, freedom, and power.

My risk was to overcome my fear and ask Joyce to marry me, knowing this was for life. It was the biggest decision I'd ever made. I secretly bought a ring and walked Joyce out to the middle of the George Washington Bridge. Standing in the gusting wind, with the mighty Hudson River flowing below us, I took my leap of faith into waters unknown to my mind but known and trusted by my heart. I asked Joyce to marry me. Physically jumping into the Hudson would not have been much harder to my then twenty-two-year-old self.

Joyce accepted. She was willing to take the risk of long-term commitment. She needed to feel my willingness to take the plunge with her. Little did I know that my plunge, my leap of faith, would lead us both into such deep fulfillment—not only in our relationship but also in our work in the world that grew out of our relationship.

Throughout our years together, there have been times when each of us has wanted to give up on the relationship. Each of those times has required another leap of faith, another plunge into the muddied waters of fear and resistance. Each time we have done this, we have gained renewed love and commitment.

It may indeed feel like the greatest of risks to dive fully into a relationship. We do sometimes risk losing our individuality, but it is the individuality of our ego wanting to keep separate for fear of being hurt, rejected, or abandoned. We can never lose our freedom unless we ourselves give it away. Ironically, through the risk of losing our individuality, we gain our true individuality, the male and female inside of us which can never be divided. When we dare to love with all our heart, we enter a paradox: What we risk to lose, we can gain even stronger. We learn to know ourselves in the full glory of our divinity.

THE FEAR OF ABANDONMENT

Why don't we human beings have more real connection with others? The reason is *fear!* We are afraid of being hurt, rejected, and abandoned. Most of us know very well the pain of being left by another person, from our earliest teen romances to marriages of many years. The more we have let ourselves become attached, the more vulnerable we have become, and the more we have felt the pain of separation. Past pain engenders more fear, and the cycle of pulling away increases.

The fear of being left needs to be looked at and confronted, not ignored. It can come up at any time and any place. One time, Joyce and I were happy finally to have a morning alone together. We planned to go for a special walk. At that point, a problem arose in the office that required more of my attention than Joyce's. One of our assistants was having trouble printing out our mailing list. I told Joyce it shouldn't take long.

A half-hour later, Joyce came into the office to check on me. She had an approaching counseling appointment and was concerned about the time. I felt I was almost done, so I asked her to wait a few more minutes. Ten more minutes passed. Joyce came in, saw I was still busy and announced, "I'm leaving now for a walk." What she felt was, "I don't want to wait any longer. If you want to come with me, it has to be now."

I had just finished at that moment so I was ready to go, but I felt hurt by Joyce's choice of words. It wasn't a big thing, but it tapped into my own unique reservoir of fear of abandonment.

We started out together on the walk. Rather than being vulnerable and expressing my hurt and, even deeper, my fear of being left, I instead criticized her for her poor choice of words. Big mistake! Joyce felt attacked and hurt and insisted on walking by herself. My fear of abandonment had just caused the very thing I was afraid of.

Here was yet another gift hiding behind the pain of relationship difficulty. I had a choice. I could push my fear of abandonment away, only to have it pop up again even stronger at another time. I could keep projecting it onto Joyce, blaming her for her ungraceful choice of words. Or instead, I could look at my ungraceful choice of actions. After all, I had in a way abandoned her by choosing our assistant's needs and the computer printer over her. Rather, I could more deeply embrace my own fear of abandonment, look at it more closely and acknowledge its presence in my personality.

Inside of every man and woman, no matter how big our bodies have grown, no matter how strong, competent, and independent we have become, resides a little child. This child does not understand logic or rationalizations and is vulnerable to all feelings, including fear, joy, anger, sadness, and love. This child needs to be held, loved, and nurtured just as much as any child we have known. We cannot ignore our inner child or the children inside those we love. To do so is to guarantee tension, distance, and arguments in the relationship.

How could I have honored my inner child in the example I just gave? Instead of directing my attention away from myself, to Joyce's use of words, I could have given expression to my inner little boy who was feeling abandoned. This would have allowed me to be more vulnerable and less attacking to Joyce. With this different approach, I may have received the love and assurance I needed. Even if I didn't receive this from Joyce, becoming vulnerable is its own reward. My inner little boy would be receiving attention and acknowledgment from my adult, nurturing self. Like a loving father reassuring a scared little boy, I could tell little Barry that I will be there for him, that I will not abandon him. Sometimes we don't get what we need from another person, at least in the moment, but we can always get what we need from within.

So, after Joyce "abandoned" me and I was left with the increased hurt of this further development, I made the choice to continue my own walk, now in the company of a little boy needing comforting. I tried my best to talk with him, to father him, and to enjoy the walk with him. After the walk, Joyce and I sat down together, aired our deeper feelings, were heard by one another, and returned to a loving feeling.

There is perhaps no deeper fear in the human experience than the fear of abandonment. We have not met anyone who does not have this fear. Many people are to some extent unconsciously ruled by it, others severely crippled by it. But everyone has this fear in various degrees and must at some time in their life confront it.

Brian, a man in a recent workshop, told the group that he had met a woman and, within a few days, had begun acting as if she were his life partner. The relationship lasted three weeks before the woman finally left him, due to the pressure she was feeling from him to be more committed than she was ready to be. In the same workshop, Alice, a middle-aged woman, described wanting to "own" men soon after meeting them. She felt unable to let a relationship evolve at its own pace.

Many people have complained to us that they choose partners who are "unavailable." Others felt they were often attracted to partners who turned out to have "too many problems." The common thread for all these people is the fear of abandonment. Brian's fear of abandonment caused him to "jump in" to the new relationship too fast, without real consideration for his own or his partner's actual readiness for long-term relationship. In fact, he shared with the group that she was newly separated and even had told him that she was not interested in a committed relationship. His fear of abandonment caused him to act in an insecure way that almost assured the outcome he most dreaded: being deserted.

Alice's fear of abandonment had caused her to compulsively cling to any man she met. Like Brian, she also was assuring relationship failure—the opposite of what she had hoped for. Her unconscious reasoning was that she's going to be rejected and abandoned anyway, so why not help the process along?

Consistently choosing unavailable partners is also an attempted defense against the pain of abandonment. If we are attracted to someone who is unavailable, this allows us to keep a "safe" distance, where we never become attached enough to be hurt by this person's leaving us.

And people who are attracted to someone who turns out to have "too many problems"? In this case, our fear of abandonment causes us to become too aware of the flaws of our partner. Our rejecting someone because of their problems is a way of not taking responsibility for our own personality defects, of not looking into the mirror of relationship to see the reflection of our own flaws. In addition, refusing to look at our reflection gives us an excuse to leave the relationship before we're abandoned. It is as if the pain of relationship loss can somehow be lessened if we can come up with a good enough reason for that loss. Blaming the separation on someone else's problems can seem the painless way out, but this ploy always backfires, and we suffer more because our fear of abandonment has operated from an unconscious and therefore more insidious place. Our fear has caused us to push away an opportunity for intimacy and joy.

Where does the fear of abandonment come from? Does it come from our childhood? It is impossible for any of us to avoid some degree of abandonment while growing up. None of us had perfect parents, attending to our every need. Most of us cried in fear and pain and the need for love, but instead may have been placed in a crib to be put to sleep, or had our diapers changed, or had a bottle or pacifier stuck in our mouth. Yet our deeper need was simply to be held and loved. No human parent can be there for us all the time, and even great parents have made mistakes that caused their children to feel the pain of rejection. This feeling of rejection is inevitable in the process of growing up. Of course, there are many whose parents were physically or emotionally present very little or not at all. These persons may have more severe problems.

In our work with the issue of abandonment, we are aware of three fundamental steps in the healing process. All of these steps involve one crucial activity, regardless of where our fear originated or how severe it is—*healing our fear of abandonment depends on our refusal to abandon ourselves.*

The first step toward healing the fear of commitment, which can be the first step to bringing more joy and love into our lives, is quite simply to become conscious of our fear of being left alone. It becomes easier to do this as we learn to accept and feel the small child within ourselves, the part that is vulnerable and scared of being abandoned. We need to also see how this fear manifests in our life and relationships. This can be a painful process, because the ego games we have previously played to protect ourselves from pain now become transparent. We can no longer pretend to be only strong, independent, and invulnerable.

Step 2 requires finding a deeper level of responsibility. It requires that we look within ourselves and discover the ways that *we abandon ourselves.* Nothing can be done about the abandonment that comes from the outside, but if we stop abandoning ourselves from within, external abandonment will not have the same influence upon us. How do we abandon ourselves? By not listening to our inner voice, the promptings of our higher knowing. By expecting our needs to be met by our partner or someone else. By not nurturing and taking care of ourselves. By not saying "No" when we need to. By giving in to feelings of unworthiness. By giving our power to our partner. By the thousands of ways we leave or ignore our own heart.

Step 3 is to stop this unhealthy process of self-abandonment. Follow a path of personal and spiritual growth, practice being gentler and kinder to yourself, and especially strive to accept and give love to your own inner child. It is easy to judge ourselves harshly when we slip into self-abandonment. As we focus more on correcting our own self-abandonment, rather than correcting everyone else's abandonment of us, we become empowered and grow in spiritual maturity. Striving to be there for ourselves rather than being preoccupied with who else is there for us, we are doing the most to heal our fear of abandonment.

THE FEAR OF COMMITMENT

So many people nowadays refer to commitment as the C word. Just mentioning the word brings a worried look to their faces. There exists that much fear of commitment.

Once, Barry and I planned to perform a wedding at the end of one of our workshops. The morning of the wedding, the groom-to-be asked with much embarrassment, "What does it mean to be committed?" Although he loved his future bride, he was confused. We shared with him what we felt to be the highest definition. To be committed to another is to keep your heart open to that person, to keep coming back to a feeling of love, to join spiritually with that person. To commit to always being together is lovely, but the highest commitment is "I will never shut you out of my heart." Likewise, to be committed to yourself is to keep your heart open to yourself, to join spiritually with yourself, to walk on the path of soul growth.

As we said before, the fear of commitment to a partner is usually the fear of becoming vulnerable and then being hurt or abandoned. There are a number of ways to heal this fear. Working with a well-recommended therapist can be a valuable tool for your growth, for shedding light on the games our egos play to keep us "safe" and separate. Participating in workshops or retreats or joining an ongoing support group can also be a way to practice taking risks to open and share yourself with others.

We have recommended to some people who found commitment particularly disturbing that they consider having a pet. It's an unusual but powerful method to help overcome fear of commitment. We have seen it work time after time.

When Rami and Mira were eleven and six, Lilly, one of our cats, had six kittens. In an attempt to find homes for them, we called all the families we knew, but no one wanted a kitten. Then we thought of a woman we knew, Ellen, who lived alone. She had once casually mentioned to us her desire to have a pet. "Let's invite her over for dinner," suggested our daughter Rami, and so we did. However, we didn't tell Ellen that it was actually going to be a blind date. After dinner, Rami and her sister Mira took Ellen to see the kittens. Mira showed her how one of the kittens had a bent tail and consequently had been named Ben. "He is a very lucky cat to have around," Mira innocently added.

We watched as Ellen fell in love with Ben and his little sister, Paws. "I've always wanted a cat," she said in a faraway tone. The desire to have a pet was there, yet the courage to take a step toward that commitment was lacking.

Rami and Mira began their gentle persuasion.

"I would have to take care of a pet every day," Ellen hesitatingly said.

"That's the best part," answered the girls. "They give you love while you care for them."

"I would need to come home from work every day to give it attention," she continued.

"When we come home from school, even if the day has been very hard, the cats make us feel happy again. Even if I didn't do well on a test," added sixth-grader Rami, "the cats cheer me up and soon I'm laughing again."

"But a cat might run away and be killed," Ellen looked sad as she spoke.

"We've had two dogs, one cat, and one kitten die," Mira offered. "They left us with happy memories."

Smiling, we left the room, leaving our friend to continue the conversation with the girls. With their childlike wisdom, they were walking this woman through her fears about committing herself to being there for another. More than talking about a pet, she was revealing her desire (and fear) about relationship.

An hour passed and Ellen emerged from the back room holding Ben in one hand and Paws in the other. She had decided to take both!

Several weeks later she called and laughingly told us of the fun she was having with the kittens. She stopped working late at her job because she was so excited to come home and play with them. Ellen eventually found a man who also liked cats, and they began dating. Their connection evolved into the first committed relationship she had ever had with a man.

Granted, there is no guarantee that caring for a pet will attract your perfect mate. Still, our family likes to think that Ben and Paws had a lot to do with healing this woman's fear of commitment and allowing her to open her heart to the beauty of relationship.

Making a commitment to an animal is making a commitment to one of God's creatures. It's a powerful step toward commitment with a person and is certainly less threatening. An animal is ever-forgiving of your personality quirks, and you are much less likely to be rejected or abandoned by an animal. Yet commitment it certainly is. Animals flourish on loving attention, and, in their innocent way, they demand it. They provide you with a continuous opportunity to give of yourself, to think of another, as well as receive the simple affection they effortlessly give.

Pets are also wonderful trainers for parenthood, the next level of commitment after relationship. Two years after getting married, we got our first pet, a Golden Retriever puppy we named Bokie. He brought our relationship to a new and heightened level of commitment. He was our first "child," and he opened our hearts to caring for others. We feel Bokie helped open the doors of our hearts to having children.

Another way to overcome fear of commitment is to spend time with a child. Children are natural teachers. Their refreshing innocence can quickly open your heart to greater love. Single parents especially need help with their children. Volunteering to spend regular time, for example, every week, with a child of a single parent is not only a service and gift to the parent, it will also provide a rich training in commitment. We suggested this method to George, a single man at one of our workshops who despaired of ever healing his fear of commitment. We then asked if there was a single mom in the group who needed help with her children. A woman immediately raised her hand. It turned out she lived close to George. He committed himself on the spot to spending at least one hour a week with her seven-year-old son. One year later, George met the woman he would marry. Did his commitment to a child lead to his commitment to a partner? In our hearts, we are convinced it helped.

THE FEAR OF BOUNDARY BLURRING

In every deep and committed love relationship, there will be times when ego boundaries are blurred and partners lose touch with where they begin and where they end. Love softens the rigidity of the ego, which tends to hold us apart from one another. To learn how to merge in love with another requires that we soften the hard edges of our being, even at the risk of blurring our boundaries. To rigidly defend our boundaries is to protect ourselves from love and growth. Better to err on the side of losing our boundaries and gaining valuable lessons about loving than to defend ourselves from love in the name of preserving our boundaries.

Yet many people are scared that love will force them to break down the barriers that keep them safe, whole, and well. In short, they fear they will have to give up themselves for love. So how do we learn the difference between opening our hearts to another and giving up on ourselves? Opening our hearts will always give us peace. Always. It may be hard to do so, especially when we feel hurt or wronged or misunderstood by the one we love. Still, when love flows, there is peace.

It is important, however, to understand the often subtle ways we blur our boundaries in an unhealthy way and therefore lose our integrity and our peace. Giving up on ourselves or not following the truth that we feel inside always results in resentment, anger, or other agitated feelings. All we have to do to prevent unhealthy boundary blurring is pay attention to how *we* feel, rather than how our partner feels or reacts. When our partner's feelings become more important than our own, we have lost a healthy boundary.

Another way we blur our boundaries is by not being in touch with the need to say "No" when it is called for. We may think we are being considerate or polite by not saying "No," but we are simply giving up on ourselves. When we say "Yes," and then feel a heaviness or a sadness, perhaps we need to listen within ourselves for the possibility that a "No" would be a more appropriate response. This is such an important topic that we have written a chapter on the importance of saying "No" later in this book.

A classic warning sign of boundary blurring is when one partner denies his or her own emotional needs to accommodate a partner. This is a form of codependence, a lack of self-respect that manifests as the "chronic giver" or "caretaker" syndrome. It is not real giving. It is only going through the motions of giving as a way of warding off the sometimes desperate need to receive. This partner denies the little child within him- or herself who deeply needs to receive love from their partner, then covers up this inner child by a facade of strength, competence, and independence. Underneath the facade, the individual is starving for love but has unconsciously given up on him- or herself. Instead of seeing their partner's needs as a reflection of their own needs, this person ignores the mirror—and by doing so, loses sense of their own boundaries.

How can you tell if you are a chronic giver in any particular situation? You will probably feel a weariness in your giving. It will tire you out because you're not taking care of your own needs. If you feel fatigue from too much giving, it's time to stop what you're doing and pay some attention to your own needs—for rest, for help, or for love.

Another of the many ways we blur our boundaries is by being a "rescuer." There is a big difference between helping our partner and rescuing them. The helper can accept their partner's emotional state, and thus give this person the space they need to recognize their condition and go through the internal steps to heal themselves. The rescuer on the other hand cannot tolerate their partner being in a negative mood and compulsively tries to change or "fix" them.

In a counseling session, a man once complained about his wife's exaggerated mood swings, especially at her premenstrual time. After he spoke, she expressed the need to simply be accepted during these times. "What I really need," she said, "is for you to see me just as I am, PMS and all. Couldn't you just hold me and let me cry and let that be OK?" He thought he was loving her by continually attempting to point out what she was doing. She felt pressured to change rather than accepted and loved. She didn't appreciate his "rescue" attempts.

In another counseling session, a woman named Rita was trying to "convince" her partner, Duane, to become more committed to the relationship. It was a difficult situation. They had conceived a child one month into their relationship, and now had a three-year-old whom they both adored. Duane, however, was feeling trapped in a relationship he felt he never consciously chose. Through her "rescuing" attempt, she was pressuring him to change rather than accepting his current feelings. By focusing so much of her energy on his lack of commitment, Rita was ignoring the reflection in the soul mirror: her own lack of commitment. In the course of the session, it became evident that Rita needed to accept her fear that he might leave her. This fear kept her from fully opening her heart to Duane. Her awareness of her part of the relationship dynamic, her own fear and lack of commitment, took the pressure off him as the only one with the problem. This allowed resolution to take place more easily.

Duane did leave for several months, then came back with a new-found commitment and enthusiasm for the relationship. He needed the time to be alone so he could make peace with himself and then actively choose the relationship. Rita needed to confront her fear of Duane leaving, as well as have her own time alone to open her heart to herself and to Duane. The time apart helped both Rita and Duane disentangle from the "rescuer-patient" relationship and establish healthy boundaries.

A good way to visualize healthy boundaries is the model of a semipermeable membrane, such as the cell membrane. It is selective and intelligent about what it lets in and out of the cell. It knows to let out the waste products of metabolism and to let in the nutrients. By giving ourselves time to be quiet, by practicing more stillness and peace, we can learn how to let in and out of our beings what we need. By giving our own feelings more validity, we can learn in each moment when and how we are blurring our boundaries in an unhealthy way and thus giving up on ourselves.

In our own relationship, there are times when love so blurs our boundaries that I don't know where I end and where Joyce begins. And the feeling is so beautiful that it doesn't matter who is who. Sometimes this happens when we meditate or pray together, sometimes when we are making love, sometimes during our workshops when we are working together. I see this as a conscious or healthy blurring of boundaries. Unlike the unhealthy form, in this situation we don't have the feeling that we are helpless or out of control. At any given moment, we can tune into our own individual selves and feel our wholeness. We feel grateful that our relationship is a safe enough place that we can let go of the walls that form impenetrable boundaries.

YES, WE CAN HEAL OUR FEARS

Susan came to see me for counseling to heal her pattern of "always getting involved with unavailable men."

"Barry," she said, "I don't get it. Why does this keep happening to me? I have such a deep longing to share my life with a man and raise a family together." She then quickly added, "Although my parents

were divorced when I was a child, I have always had a close relationship with each of them as individuals."

I felt a need to ask her a question. "Susan, what are you afraid of?"

Without hesitation, she blurted out, "I'm afraid of getting too
close to another person. I'm afraid of relationship."

I asked Susan to close her eyes and check if any images or feelings came to her about this fear. After a moment of silence, she
painfully remembered the last argument her parents had before they
finally separated and later divorced. She opened her eyes and
described the scene to me.

"I'm five years old and standing in the living room looking into
the kitchen, where my parents are arguing. My mother's boyfriend is
waiting outside in a car. I can hear him beep the horn. My father is
trying to prevent my mother from leaving."

Tears then welled up in her eyes, and she looked at me and said,
"The memory hurts too much. I have to stop."

I explained to her that part of her healing lay in consciously
returning to that painful scene, re-experiencing all the feelings. No
explanation of what happened could really benefit her because the
original trauma was on a feeling, experiential level. It was not a mental concept. I asked for her willingness and she agreed to try.

I had her close her eyes again and coached her in deep breathing
as a way to move more deeply into her body and feelings. I asked her
to once again become that five-year-old girl standing in her living
room and describe what she was experiencing.

In a moment, she began speaking. She could see her mother's
boyfriend waiting outside in his car. Her mother was getting ready to
leave, while her father followed her around begging her to stay. He
had tears in his eyes. Susan's mother kept saying "No" to him. Their
voices grew louder and angrier. They yelled awful things at each
other. Her father grabbed her mother's arm, trying to keep her from
leaving. Susan cowered in the corner, terrified of what was going to
happen next.

Suddenly it was over. Susan's father let go of her mother's arm. He
ordered her to leave and never come back.

Susan burst into tears as she remembered her mother coming over to her to say good-bye. She was crying and holding her tightly. "It was very scary," said Susan. "I didn't know if I'd ever see my mom again."

Still crying, but now with her eyes open, Susan shared that the worst part of the whole experience was her feeling of helplessness. All five-year-old Susan could do was stand there by herself and cry.

I knew there was only one thing to do. I told her, "Susan, you need to return to that traumatic scene, not as a helpless child but as a powerful woman who can speak her truth."

The look she gave me clearly said, "You can't be serious," yet she also sensed the need for this return and the potential for healing.

She closed her eyes once more. I guided her back to her place in the living room. I spoke to her gently but firmly, reminding Susan that she is an adult now, that she could now call upon an abundance of help. "Go ahead. Feel the presence of all those who have ever loved you throughout your life, and draw strength from their love."

This time, Susan sat with her eyes closed for several minutes. I remained quiet, giving her the time to do what she needed to do. I watched a smile come to her face, and soon her eyes opened. There was peace and also power in her eyes as she reported, "I stepped between my parents while they were yelling at one another, looked at them both, and commanded them to stop acting so immaturely. When they quieted down, I was able to then share my pain and fear with them. They actually listened." Susan also shared her love with her parents and, because of this love, she could see the wisdom in their need to separate. "However painful," she added, "I could see the deep growth that was coming to all of us."

Now Susan was beaming! She said, "I feel like a huge weight has been lifted from my heart. All these years, the trauma of that memory and my parent's divorce has been blocking me and my relationships. I've never made the connection, or saw how much I feared the same kind of painful separation happening to me. That must be why I get involved with 'unavailable' men."

Through her willingness to confront her fears, Susan took a giant step in her growth. She came to a place in her life where she was unwilling to be dominated by what she recognized as unhealthy patterns in her relationships.

Each of us can learn from Susan. We all have, to various degrees, unhealthy patterns that seem to unconsciously have a hold on us. It's important to remember that these patterns may have their origin in a painful or traumatic experience, whether in our recent or distant past. If we desire healing, we must first become aware of those unhealthy patterns—regardless of their origin. We can sometimes do this by using methods of inner work like prayer or meditation. Sometimes we need professional help.

Most importantly, we need the courage and the willingness to *feel our feelings* underlying the pattern. Only then can we move through it. It is not always necessary to uncover the exact cause or situation, or from when and where the trauma came. In fact, this can sometimes lead to a fruitless mental search. In fact, the wisdom of Susan's healing has less to do with her discovery of the source of her pain than with her ability to love and forgive.

Through all the work we have done with people's fears, we have learned that it can be a trap simply to blame our family of origin for our fear of abandonment or for any of our dysfunction. To blame our parents for our own issues is similar to blaming our lover for the problems in our relationship. To do so is to avoid looking into the mirror and taking responsibility for our own spiritual evolution. Our childhood experiences are valid. They happened, and affected us deeply, but our souls are bigger than the effects of our childhood, and we are more than a product of our growing up. *We are vast, spiritual beings, taking on experience in multidimensional ways. The reach of our souls is far greater than anything we can sense with our rational, intellectual minds. Life is bigger, and runs deeper, than the events which shape our personalities.*

True healing can only happen on the heart or spiritual level. True healing requires us to accept all of our feelings, all of our fears, rather than merely figuring out the origin of our unhealthy patterns as if we were solving a math problem. Being able to accept our feelings and experiences is the real adventure of healing, the excitement of self-discovery, and the journey to the highest love possible.

HEALING OUR FEARS

In what ways does intimate relationship scare you? This is a good time to take inventory of those fears. Are you afraid of losing your power—or losing your sense of self? How about a fear of abandonment or rejection? Has commitment been difficult for you? Do you have trouble setting clear boundaries for yourself, and are therefore afraid of getting too close to another?

Now envision yourself as more than a collection of fears. You are bigger than your fears. Feel your fears. Watch your fears. Even play with your fears if you want to. They are separate from the real you.

Breathe into and out of the center of your chest, your heart area. A light perpetually shines there but, when your attention is on your fear, you are not aware of this light. Concentrate all of your attention now upon this light shining from your heart. Visualize or feel its brightness, its warmth, its profound peace. Fear is like a gray morning fog obscuring this light. Love, the essence of who you are, is like the sun's rays which finally penetrate even the densest fog and bring the bright colors back to the world.

10

From Codependence to Interdependence

Whether a room has been dark for one night or a hundred years, the room is just as bright when a candle is lit.

—RAMAKRISHNA

CODEPENDENCE AND INTERDEPENDENCE are at the opposite ends of the spectrum of need in relationship. Codependence implies unconscious need or dependence upon another person, and is thus often expressed in an unhealthy way. It is a refusal to acknowledge our psychological dependence upon another. In order to mature spiritually, to attain spiritual greatness, we must realize our interdependence, the awareness of our *healthy* need for one another. Embracing our interdependence brings more love into all of our relationships.

We once worked with a couple who revealed a classic example of codependence. Gary was a daily marijuana user. Like many people addicted to a substance, he denied his addiction. He felt he used marijuana as a tool to help him in his creative endeavors. However, as we wrote in *Risk to Be Healed*, we have learned that marijuana or any other mind-altering substance only gives the illusion or approximation of heightened creativity or consciousness. Its actual effect is to dampen consciousness by placing a filter over it, while often leaving the person more dependent on the substance.

Gary's wife, Ann, expressed a strong resentment toward her husband's habit, which she saw as destroying their relationship. She, however, felt powerless to take a strong stand about this issue. When we coached her deeper into her feelings, she finally became aware of her side of their mutual codependence—her addiction to their sexual relationship. Sex to Ann was not very different than marijuana was to Gary. Each had their own habit, but in the classical sense (and original definition) of codependence, these two addictions were mutually supportive. In their codependence, Gary and Ann were in some ways reflections of each other, two sides of the same coin. They fed off one another. They "enabled" each other. The more Gary indulged in pot smoking, the more unconscious he became in his relating with Ann, including not being fully present during sex. This triggered her own insecurity, including her fear of abandonment, which plunged her further into sex as an artificial "fix" rather than an expression of intimacy. And the more Ann gave in to her sex addiction, the more dulled her own consciousness became, the more separate she became from Gary, and the more he smoked in a mostly unconscious effort to escape the pain of this separation. And on and on it goes.... This is the dance of codependence.

An important aspect of the journey of relationship involves first the recognition of our codependence and then our acceptance of it. For each of us to accept our codependence is to accept a part of our humanity, rather than to judge it, make it wrong, or push it away, which keeps it buried and unconscious. The acceptance of our codependence humbles us and can lead to our awareness of healthy dependence, which we refer to as interdependence.

There is a vast difference between feeling our need for another (an aspect of interdependence) and expecting or demanding another to fill that need (an aspect of codependence). Interdependence implies taking responsibility for our feelings, desires, and actions.

When we don't take responsibility for ourselves, a codependent inter-action is the result. One classic example is the man who gets angry at his wife because he can't find his favorite socks. In his unconscious mind, he is wanting and expecting his wife (Mommy) to take care of him. If he recognizes his projection onto his wife and accepts the part of him that needs to be taken care of by her, he can relax more in the "sock" interaction. He can even find joy in his inner child's need for "Mommy." When there is a feeling of joy or peace mixed in with our feeling of need for another, we are touching upon interdependence and healing our codependence.

Another example of codependence is the mother who com-plains to her grown children that they don't telephone her enough. Her complaining is an unconscious cover-up for her need for their love and attention. If she can be more emotionally honest and sim-ply share her need for love, her honesty will give her the best pos-sible chance of receiving what she needs. More important, if she can be at peace with her need for love, she will heal her codependent actions.

Our codependence can often be traced to our inner child's need for love, our fear of that need, and our protective mechanism (the sock man's anger and the mother's complaining) to keep this vulnera-ble child hidden from view—and therefore protected from possible hurt or rejection. The healing comes when we find the courage to look at our vulnerable inner child and accept and make peace with the love that child needs.

It is healthy to feel our physical, emotional, psychological, and spiritual needs for others. This represents a humble acceptance of where we stand as human beings. It is unhealthy, however, to project those needs onto someone else and expect or demand that they do something about them. This projection is manipulative and is the root of codependent behavior as well as many other relationship prob-lems. It is, at least in part, looking outside of ourselves for the source of our happiness. We will never find it out there. The healthy posi-tion is to feel both our human need for love as well as the divine source of that love in ourselves and in others.

We need to be honest with ourselves about our codependence, our unhealthy ways of relating. Yet our eventual healing and fulfillment lies in accepting our interdependence, the awareness that we are not alone on this planet. We need each other very much. Our survival as a species depends on our interdependence. We can only survive through love and cooperation—and acceptance of our need for one another as well as our need to give to one another.

The journey from codependence to interdependence has been important in my relationship with Joyce. In our early relationship, our codependence was a hidden monster waiting to rear its ugly head whenever we allowed our denial to put us to sleep. I fell asleep through denial of the human part of me (little Barry) that was dependent on Joyce. For me at that time, to need another person was a statement of weakness and insecurity, not very desirable qualities. And so, by feeling this way, it became easy to split off this needy child part of me into an unconscious realm. It became easy to fool myself into thinking I had no need for Joyce, that I was free of attachment to her. I was addicted to the myth of my independence, denying my fear of dependence and abandonment.

Joyce, on the other hand, fell asleep in our early relationship through denial of the strength of her intuition. She tended to come to me to help her solve problems and understand other people's actions toward her. She turned to me rather than her own inner wisdom for the guidance and direction she needed in her life. Her feeling of overdependence was a mirror image of my feeling of underdependence. It was hard for her to feel this much dependence, especially when it appeared to so contrast with my apparent lack of dependence. In reaction to the unacceptability of these feelings, she also unconsciously hid them away from her awareness.

Our polarization might have continued for a long time. But then something happened. By the middle of my second year of medical school in Nashville, Tennessee, Joyce and I had been married for one year. A friend excitedly told us that a former teacher of hers was about to visit from Los Angeles. She invited us to a party she was having for him. The man's name was Leo Buscaglia, now the author of many popular books about love. We were in no way prepared for that party.

Within minutes after arriving, this middle-aged man with sparkly eyes and a smile almost as big as he was embraced Joyce and me in the kind of hug that we usually reserved for the oldest and dearest friends, and then only after not seeing one another for a long time. Remember that all this took place at a time when hugging was not yet the norm. The thought of the President of the United States hugging the Vice President would have been unthinkable. To say that Leo's hug stretched us beyond our limits is an understatement.

It was the beginning, however, of a new phase in our lives, a deep plunge into the open sharing of love with those outside of our relationship. This plunge was a blessing, for we learned how to open our hearts wider to others. As a couple, we had previously been rather private with our love and innermost thoughts and feelings. In some ways, this period in our lives was a foundation for the work we now do with our writing, speaking, and workshops.

It was also a challenge, especially for me. For someone in denial about his own emotional needs for others, the sharing of love can present a problem. I have to admit that I was not very mature at that time of my life. I had difficulty taking responsibility for being in a committed relationship. I was afraid of losing my freedom, of being held captive in the prison that I perceived some relationships had become. I was big on freedom in those days—at least in the outward expression. Inwardly, I was far from free, only I didn't know it. Of course, underlying my fear of losing my freedom was my real fear, that of coming too close to another (Joyce), my fear of intimacy, vulnerability, and dependence, and my fear of rejection and abandonment. In my unconscious reasoning, if I had more than one close relationship, the fear and pain of abandonment by one of them would be diminished. Unfortunately, it doesn't work that way. In trying to protect myself from pain, I was instead protecting myself from love.

So, as I rationalized, that first hug from Leo gave me permission to become involved with other women in the name of freedom and love. This was not at all what Leo was teaching. He was teaching the free expression of love and caring, but because of my unconscious need for love (my codependence), I misinterpreted the message as a way to run away from commitment and intimacy with Joyce.

Needless to say, it was a painful time, but also a time of much growth. It was a time of waking up from my sleep of denial about my inner child's need for love. Previously, I projected my own inner child onto Joyce, seeing only her need for love and dependence upon me. Now, I was learning to see Joyce as a soul mirror, reflecting back to me my own inner child needing so much love. I began to see this need, and my inner child, as something that has always been with me, as something that is healthy and positive. I began to realize that my inner child, if I let it, would not only teach me about my need for love from Joyce, but also my need for love from all of creation. I was awakening to the reality of my codependence, an awakening that would in turn lead me to an awareness of my interdependence, my interconnectedness with everyone and everything.

When we touch upon this great awareness of our interdependence, a light is also shed upon our codependence. It cannot remain hidden from our sight. Our connection with Leo and other important friends at that time, while being a powerful force for opening our hearts, also magnified the unhealthy aspects of our relationship. When you turn on the lights of a house brightly enough, the light eventually finds its way into the dark, hidden closets and illuminates their contents as well. So it is with the dark places in our souls. The light must penetrate all of these places if we are to be free.

For my final two years of medical school, we moved to Los Angeles, where I attended the University of Southern California. Joyce was awarded a scholarship for a master's degree program in USC's Department of Child Psychology. And who was one of her main preceptors? Leo Buscaglia! We even stayed at his house our first week in L.A., until we discovered an apartment for rent three houses down the street.

Leo had a profound influence upon our lives those next two years. His message to those of us who were close to him was always simple—come into your heart, come into love, and see through the illusions of our existence to the beauty of life. And when we were around him, it seemed that life was full of magic. Of course, we all attributed much of the magic to Leo and didn't realize it was in each one of us, that it was in the chemistry of being together, sharing that heart space, sharing an atmosphere of love.

One night I had a powerful dream. I was standing in a dark room, aware of many others in the room, but couldn't see anyone. Leo was in the middle of the room standing at some kind of altar. He seemed to be focused on trying to do something. Finally, a small glowing light appeared on the altar. It was slowly growing in intensity, then suddenly exploded into a blinding white light. I let out a yell and jumped up in bed, waking Joyce in the process. It was my first dream of the power of the "Great White Light" spoken about in many traditions and I wasn't spiritually ready for the experience. It overwhelmed me.

Several days later, Leo visited us at our apartment. I told him about the dream. He sat upright suddenly, eyes open wide. He excitedly told us that he'd been having the same dream. Three nights in a row, he stood at the same altar, in the same dark room, kindling a small light. In the dream, he felt somewhat sad that no one seemed to be able to see it. The third and final night of his dream was the night I had mine. Now he knew his work had not been in vain.

The three of us sat there entranced with one another, letting the meaning of the dream sink in. We were deeply moved by the profound connection we had. We felt the sacred privilege that was ours in sharing this Light.

This is the heart of interdependence. The light of love is passed from human heart to human heart and becomes like a string of living pearls. Our times of solitude are important not as times when we are separate, but as times when we feel our connection with all of creation. Then, our times with our fellow human travelers on this path can also be more fulfilling. The deepest need of the soul is to give and receive of the nectar called love.

FROM CODEPENDENCE TO INTERDEPENDENCE

There is a little child inside you who needs love, approval, acknowledgment, and much more. Take time to ponder and feel the needs of this inner child. Realize there is nothing wrong with having this child and these needs. If the adult, conscious part of you doesn't accept these needs and this inner child, the energy will instead be expressed as fear, anger, manipulation, clinging, or a host of other codependent ways that only cover up the deeper needs.

Let yourself also feel your interdependence, your thread in the great tapestry of life, your place in all of creation. You need others. Others need you. You have much to give to life and much to receive from life.

Now imagine or feel a great light all around and within you, cradling your inner child with unconditional love. This light is taking care of your inner child. Relax. You don't have to work so hard to protect the vulnerable part of you. You need only to receive the nurturing of this divine presence. This light is ever-present and ever waiting for your willingness to receive the love you deserve.

11

Learning from the Mirror

You who want knowledge,
seek the Oneness within.
There you will find
the clear mirror already waiting.

—HADEWIJCH II

S WE JOURNEY ON OUR SPIRITUAL PATH, various issues
come up, issues that must be confronted if we are to
flourish. Some of the issues we'll discuss in this chapter
are ones we see over and over in our counseling and
workshops. Some are more unusual but are included because of the
important soul lessons they teach. Some are responses to questions
that were sent to us from all over the country by people trying to
make their relationships work better. Each illustrates another facet of
the "soul mirror" path to spiritual growth—the magical process
whereby every problem in a relationship gives you a chance to look
more deeply at yourself. For if we scratch below the surface of every
difficulty, we will find an opportunity for growth. But first, to help
you understand how relationships provide us with a soul mirror, you

might want to meditate on the following practice before you read further.

BEHOLD THE MIRROR

Sit quietly by yourself. Breathe deeply to help still your mind and relax your body.

What qualities of your partner (or someone you love) do you have difficulty with? What do they do (or not do) that you simply cannot ignore? Take the time to see and feel this as clearly as you can.

Now imagine this person lifting up a panel of slightly mirrored glass in front of their face. You can still see their face through the glass, but if you shift your focus, you can instead see your own face. So, with only a slight shift of focus, you realize you are looking into a mirror at your own face rather than through clear glass at another's face. This is a critical part of the visualization practice. It will help you take responsibility for what you are projecting onto another, to reclaim those qualities that also belong to you.

At this point, you need to feel your willingness to grow and to learn the soul lessons this particular mirror has to offer. You need to be different from the vain queen in *Snow White* who refused to accept the truth of the magic mirror. You are being asked now to reclaim all your projections.

Pick one quality or behavior in your loved one's personality that you find difficult to accept. Examine closely the feelings or thoughts evoked in you by this particular quality or behavior. These are your own feelings or thoughts. They are perhaps triggered by another person, but nonetheless they are yours.

The key to your growth is looking carefully now at what you find unacceptable in *yourself*, rather than what is unacceptable in another person. Remember, what you don't like "out there" is really showing you something that you don't like within yourself. It may be the same quality or behavior in yourself, or it may be something different but brought up by this person's personality. You may find a dysfunction within you that is complementary to a loved one's dysfunction. Yet, for your own growth, it is imperative that you discover your own contribution to the dysfunction in the relationship.

In a similar way, is there a "positive" projection, a strength or beauty you attribute only to the other person, a way that you put this person onto a pedestal, higher than yourself? This, too, will keep you from true closeness.

Have the courage to look deeply into the mirror. If you do, you will find something that needs love and acceptance within yourself. Then give yourself this love and acceptance, and watch your relationship grow and evolve as well.

THE INSENSITIVE PARTNER

The following letter from a woman illustrates the soul mirror at work and how to use it effectively for our own spiritual growth and the growth of our relationships:

"When I fell in love with Ethan, I was thrilled to finally meet a man who was truly sensitive. Ethan had worked hard on himself. He had been in therapy for seven years, he had started a men's support group, and he had actually made peace with his two ex-wives and countless ex-girlfriends. Now, after two years of marriage, I feel he is still sensitive and considerate of everyone—except me. He seems more sensitive to his ex-wife, Patty, his ex-girlfriends, and even his mother. This concerns me deeply. We have a one-year-old daughter and he is great with her. How can I get him to be as sensitive to my needs as he used to be? I still love him very much but often feel hurt, confused, and frustrated because of this. I sometimes feel like I'm the last one on his sensitivity list."

Here, we have a classic example of projecting onto another what needs to be seen within. What we said to her was this: "Perhaps the biggest step you can take in the healing of your relationship is to focus on your own insensitivity rather than Ethan's. Sure, your husband's insensitivity may be much more apparent to you than your own, but that doesn't mean he has the only problem in this area. We're not implying he doesn't have a problem with insensitivity to you. The point is, the more you try to work on his insensitivity, the more you try to get Ethan to be more respectful and considerate of you, the worse it may become because you are ignoring your *own* insensitivity.

"Here's the way the paradox of soul-mirroring works: *You have been insensitive to his sensitivity toward you.* It's like seeing a glass as half-empty rather than half-full. It's a matter of perspective. Understanding the mirror of relationship is a matter of accepting a new and deeper paradigm. You need to develop a more profound understanding of the true source of your own happiness. You will grow spiritually by taking personal responsibility for your own peace and the peace in your relationships.

"And just how can you be more sensitive to Ethan? The most obvious way to us is to look for and see the ways he is sensitive to you. We are convinced there are times when Ethan is considerate of your needs. Rather than complaining about how rare these occasions may be, you have the wonderful opportunity of carefully watching for such moments. And believe us, your attentiveness in this way will allow you to see your husband's sensitivity more than you ever have.

"Then, when you do see a show of respect or sensitivity to you, however small, acknowledge and enjoy it as much as you can, without any expectation that doing this will change him. If it feels appropriate, sincerely appreciate Ethan for his consideration of you. But this verbal or outward appreciation can be a little tricky. It may be better to appreciate your husband inwardly rather than outwardly. Your appreciation will have the same effect of cultivating his sensitivity toward you, without the possibility of his defensiveness or perhaps his feeling that you are acting in a condescending manner toward him. Even more, by focusing on his sensitivity toward you, you will be cultivating your own sensitivity—toward yourself as well as your husband. And this is your work on a soul level, *becoming the very thing you want from your beloved.*

"You mentioned Ethan is great with your little daughter. Here is yet another opportunity for you to practice appreciating him. Let him know how good he is with her and how grateful you are for this. It will not only make him better with her, it will also draw him closer to you."

Insensitivity is simply a habit we get ourselves into. As soon as we human beings get comfortable in a particular situation, we start to take it for granted. As long as our bodies are healthy, for example, we tend to forget about them. We lose awareness of their preciousness. Then, we get sick or have an accident. The result is increased sensitivity and appreciation. How much better to give thanks for our health every day, rather than waiting for sickness to awaken our appreciation.

The same is true of our relationships. As we get secure and comfortable with our partner, as we become more and more predictable to each other, we tend to "fall asleep" in relationship. We begin to bury the flame of divine passion. The habitual patterns of our daily lives can easily dull our sensitivity to one another. Then something drastic may happen, something that threatens our relationship. The result of this shaking up is a waking up, with increased sensitivity and appreciation.

If we want our relationships to soar in the highest way, if we want the deepest level of respect, intimacy, and trust, we need to give thanks and appreciation every day. Know that sensitivity is something that can be cultivated. Some of us feel that if we appreciate another, we will somehow lose our own self-esteem. Not so. For, as we have explained, what you see or project outwardly is magically what you become. If you focus your attention on love, inside or outside, you surely and steadily become love yourself. All it takes is loving attention to our soul mirrors.

DIFFERENCES IN EMOTIONAL EXPRESSION

"It seems Caroline is weaker than me," said Joseph in a counseling session. "All I have to do is look at her wrong and she's in tears. And the tiniest things seem to upset her. When we first met, she seemed to have it so much more together. Now I find myself spending a lot of time having to comfort her when she's emotionally upset. I'm afraid I'm losing respect for Caroline."

To begin with, Joseph has made the assumption that showing emotion is a sign of weakness. Perhaps Caroline is very emotionally expressive, but this is often a natural reaction to a partner who exhibits the other extreme, the unconscious repression or holding in of emotion. This dynamic—a man who is not fully aware of his emotions bonded to a woman who appears to be overexpressive of her emotions—is a typical one, although some couples manifest the reverse—the overemotional man and underemotional woman.

A major lesson for Joseph in his relationship was to become aware of his feelings. Until he was, his partner might be the only one who seemed "untogether." Because of Joseph's fear and avoidance of his own emotionality, and seeing it as a weakness, he attributed both emotionality and weakness to the one he loved. During the counseling session, he came to see that Caroline's "weakness" was actually her strength and that his "strength" was actually his weakness. He understood the work on himself he needed to do to uncover his emotions.

I remember having this same judgment about Joyce. Little by little, over the years, I have grown to appreciate the wisdom in Joyce's wide range of emotional expression. Whereas I used to be offended by her sudden (and unexpected) show of emotion, now I try to use it as a clue to what I need to learn in a particular situation. Often now, I feel grateful (although sometimes not at the time) for the way Joyce becomes a teacher for me.

Growing up as a boy in this culture, I quickly got the message that expression of feelings (any feelings!) got one labeled as a "sissy" or a weakling. Then, starting in the '60s, I learned that feeling my feelings gave me my deepest strength. Now is the time for integration. Thinking and feeling are equally important. Thought is like a vessel that can contain feeling; Feeling can give added life to thought. Both are equally beautiful, and they can coexist in a delightful balance.

So one partner is not more together just because they are more aware of emotion, nor is the other partner more together because of their "level-headedness." The real "togetherness" comes from the balance of the two qualities within us and within our beloved. And this is why we are in relationship—so we can look into the soul mirror of our partner and honor what is really within ourselves, and thus learn from each other and bring emotional balance into our lives.

MENTAL-EMOTIONAL BALANCING

Either sit facing each other or close your eyes and visualize your partner.

Do you sometimes judge yourself as being too emotional or not emotional enough?

Do you judge yourself as expressing your feelings too much or not enough? Being too much or too little in your head, in your rational thinking mind?

Do you sometimes judge your partner in the same way?

Remember when you were younger, much younger.
Remember a time when you were balanced mentally and

emotionally, when it was a thrill to think creative thoughts *and* to feel many different feelings.

The capacity for full, creative thinking and feeling are still within you. Seeing one quality as more developed in your partner is ignoring that quality present in yourself, although perhaps more hidden from your view. Try to acknowledge that quality in yourself. It is there. It just needs more of your attention.

Likewise, seeing one quality as less developed in your partner is not seeing your partner deeply enough. If your partner appears to you as not thinking clearly enough or not feeling enough, it is time for you to look at the judgment you have about thinking and feeling, and the lack of balance of these two qualities *within yourself*. As you honor both qualities within yourself, you will behold them in your partner, and your relationship will become more balanced.

SLOW IS NOT BAD

While working with Pam and Mark in psychotherapy, I became aware of an interesting pattern. Pam was frustrated with Mark's slowness in processing emotions, especially during a disagreement or when feelings were hurt. During these times, she was able to zip along a chain of related feelings with great speed, interspersing these feelings with questions to Mark to try to get him to somehow speed up his "emotional processor." He felt like he was trying to keep up with a Ferrari while driving a Volkswagen, which added to his shame and feelings of inadequacy.

I reflected that I too was slower than Joyce in processing and integrating feelings. I asked Mark, "Is there any way that Pam is slower that frustrates you?"

He thought for a while, then answered, "Yes—skiing! I love the feeling of the wind on my face as I sail dancing down the hills. I wish Pam could keep up with me. I have to continually stop and wait for her to catch up."

"Anything else?" I asked.

"Yes, I just thought of another example. Figuring things out. It sometimes frustrates me to wait for her to find someplace on a map, or figure out instructions to how something works."

Evidently, Pam was in general slower than Mark at processing outer physical or mental expression, like physical coordination or external logic. Mark was slower than Pam at processing internal expression. These differences are not uncommon.

Mark and Pam could just as easily have been Barry and Joyce. We fit this pattern too, which from time to time has caused us some conflict. At times, I have felt frustrated with Joyce's slowness in certain physical or mental areas, and she has felt frustrated with my slowness in certain emotional arenas.

However, it is too simplistic to generalize. There have been times when I have been impatient with Joyce's slowness in working through a hurt or resentment involving another person. And there have been times when Joyce has been impatient with my slowness in making decisions.

Our frustration, impatience, or lack of acceptance of a quality in our lover reflects back to us these same feelings about ourselves. When I feel frustrated with Joyce's slowness, I am conveniently avoiding my frustration with my own slowness.

Each of us, whether woman or man, is slow in some ways and fast in other ways. Our relationships teach us that we are drawn to a partner who is compatible with us. This means we have some things to teach our partner and other things to learn.

We need to get clear about our judgmental attitudes. *Judging another is really judging ourselves. Wanting another to change is wanting ourselves to change.* Next time you point your finger at your beloved, look more closely at your hand. Three fingers are pointing back at you, reminding you to take responsibility for what you behold in the mirror of relationship.

Rather than making a judgment, we can understand that fast is not always better than slow. In any particular area of the relationship, it doesn't necessarily mean the person who is faster is the better teacher. Regarding the ski slope, I reminded Mark that his real desire was for connection with Pam, more than the rush of speeding down the hill. By slowing down and pacing himself with Pam, he could be dancing with *her* instead of the air. *And* he might be able to put more consciousness into each movement, making skiing more of a meditation.

Equally, just because Pam is faster processing emotion doesn't mean she is Mark's teacher in this area. In fact, her frustration reveals the ways she needs to grow herself and shows that she is not honoring Mark's process. She wants him to be different than he is. Again, fast is not better than slow. Pam's goal, too, is connection with Mark, not competition with him or getting him to change. For her to slow down her internal mental and emotional processes, to breathe more deeply to allow some space between the rapid succession of thoughts and feelings, would allow her a greater chance of joining Mark. She would also have more peacefulness and enjoyment in the process.

Each one of us needs to honor our own slowness, not as a sign of weakness or retardation, but as a gift in our lives. When we are critical of our own slowness, we will probably be critical of our partner's slowness. When we accept our own slowness, we learn to see the beauty of our partner's slowness. Most of us simply move too fast in our lives. Far too many children seem to be in a hurry to grow up. The pace of technological breakthroughs is heightening. But peace is found only by slowing down, not hurrying up. When we slow down our minds, we enjoy life more. When we slow down our bodies (for example, through T'ai Chi) we enjoy each movement more. When we accept the gift of whatever slowness we possess, we can accept our partner's slowness, and we will feel a deeper connection with ourselves and with our partner.

WIN-WIN DECISION MAKING

Decision making can be a difficult area of relationship, especially when decisions touch upon sensitive issues such as money, disciplining children, in-laws, complications from a former marriage—the list could go on and on. Yet decision making can also be an opportunity for two people to grow closer to one another in understanding. It all depends upon how they approach the process. A decision of any kind must be approached with sensitivity to the feelings of all involved. *Each person must feel that his or her opinion is wanted, respected, and absolutely necessary.* Barry and I have seen problems in relationships where one person goes ahead and makes a decision that affects the other without consulting him or her. This makes the ignored person feel that his or her feelings are not important or valued. No one likes to feel left out or unimportant. If you are ever in doubt as to whether or not to ask your partner's advice about a decision—*ask!*

Once you've asked their opinion, what happens if your thinking conflicts? It is important then to stop and ask yourself, "Do I really want to hear their feelings on this subject, or do I want to convince him or her of my opinion?" If the latter is true, then it is time to sit back and listen some more. No good decision in a relationship is ever made by one person deciding and the other merely complying. In fact, this is a recipe for disaster. In good decision making in a relationship, there is no such thing as one person winning. That creates a loser, which in turn creates resentment. The partner who "wins" a decision eventually finds that they loses in the overall scheme of the relationship. There is a great saying: *A person can either choose to be right, or they can choose love.* If the choice is love, then each person must be carefully listened to, considered, and valued. In this way, the decision becomes a joint effort which will serve the relationship.

Partners often approach a decision in different ways. This is one of the beauties of relationship, adding variety and balance. Honoring each person's process is important in making decisions. Perhaps one partner is more intellectual, making decisions from facts, information, and knowledge about a topic. Often, in balance, the other partner is more intuitive, sometimes completely ignoring the "facts." This process can be rather frustrating to the more intellectual partner, just as the intellectual process can be frustrating to the intuitive partner. However, the rational person needs to realize they were attracted to their partner for perhaps this very reason, and their rational brain sometimes needs the balance of the heart's nonlinear approach. Likewise, the intuitive person at times needs a more rational approach to a decision. Both are necessary and, when each is honored, decision making can be a truly wonderful way to grow in closeness and respect.

The key here is honoring one another's differences instead of trying to change each other. Honoring your beloved's approach to decision making is honoring yourself—and your own approach—as well. Make room in your relationship for differences, so the similarities can shine even brighter. Respect what is different about your beloved, and you will unite in a deeper way.

When difficult decisions have to be made, remember to acknowledge first your own decision to be fully present in this relationship. Remember the feeling of rightness and the inner knowing of love and respect. If you can approach decisions from a place of honoring your connection, then those decisions will serve to bring your relationship into ever greater heights.

THE SPHERE OF COMMITMENT

Kevin and Marsha did not look like "happy campers" as they sat down for a counseling session. For two and a half years, Kevin had been having a "strictly nonsexual" relationship with another woman, Michele. He had trouble understanding why Marsha felt so jealous of Michele. Why wasn't it acceptable for him to have a friend of the opposite sex, especially if that friendship didn't take him away from his wife? His position seemed innocent enough.

Then I turned my attention to Marsha. She felt insecure in the relationship, that it was all her problem. "If only I weren't so jealous of Kevin's attention going to another woman, Barry," she said with her head hung low, "I'd be able to be more open to Kevin when he does show me love."

I asked Kevin, "What are you getting from your relationship with Michele?"

He thought for a moment, then replied, "It's an easy relationship. We share a deep, spiritual connection without any conflict. We're good friends. I'm not attracted to her sexually. We're just good friends."

Then I asked, "What about Marsha?"

Kevin glanced at Marsha hesitatingly. I encouraged him to be completely honest.

"I'm sexually attracted to Marsha and want to stay married to her," he started, "but the relationship seems so difficult."

Later in the session, it became evident that the relationship with Michele was an exclusive relationship. Kevin revealed how important it was for him to be alone with Michele. Though it wasn't sexual, Kevin was making no room for Marsha in his relationship with Michele, so it was clearly taking Kevin away from his marriage. That's why she felt insecure and jealous. In effect, Kevin was having a personal and intimate relationship, an affair, with Michele even though they never had sex.

I looked at the two of them while they continued sharing their problems. I was noticing the lack of real commitment in their relationship when an interesting image came to me. I sensed a "place" or focus of commitment located between the two, almost as an indicator of where their mutual concern lay. This sphere of commitment seemed to reside not centrally between the two, but rather about a foot from Kevin's head. In other words it was skewed, much closer to Kevin than to Marsha.

I told Marsha and Kevin about the image and how I felt their commitment was unbalanced. Kevin's commitment was more to himself, to his own truth, his own happiness and well-being. Of course this kind of commitment is necessary, but it was unbalanced because of his lack of concern for Marsha's happiness and growth. Marsha's commitment was more to Kevin. She was more concerned about being with him than with herself. Being a devoted wife was outweighing her own self-respect.

They sat there sadly nodding their heads in agreement and said they never saw their lack of balance so clearly. It's not that Kevin shouldn't be totally committed to his own happiness. A deep commitment to loving oneself is necessary for a relationship to work, but there needs to be just as strong a commitment to be sensitive to the needs of one's partner. Similarly, it's not wrong for Marsha to be so devoted to Kevin. Her sensitivity to his needs is also a powerful tool for their relationship, but if she is ignoring her own needs and not respecting her own truth, the relationship cannot flourish. It's a sensitive balancing act. Too much attention to self is self-centered; too much attention to others can be codependent. If the relationship is to work, the "sphere of commitment" needs to hover centrally between the two partners—in balance.

If Kevin can acknowledge Marsha as a soul mirror, he will see his own concern and consideration for her through the image and reflection of her attention to him. His commitment to Marsha is somewhat hidden to Kevin, but is nonetheless there. This commitment to Marsha, someone outside of himself, can become visible—if he accepts that Marsha is reflecting it back to him.

Likewise, it is important that Marsha accept Kevin as a soul mirror. He is reflecting the commitment to herself that Marsha needs to see. This is the mirror image of Kevin's involvement with himself.

Over the years, I've been sensitive to the lack of balance of the "sphere of commitment" even though I've never before been able to articulate it quite in these terms. In our early relationship, Joyce was Marsha and I was Kevin. Our "sphere of commitment" was similarly lopsided. As I have been accepting Joyce as a soul mirror, I have been learning how to devote myself unconditionally to her well-being without leaving my center of self-respect. In fact, whenever I do something with the intention of making Joyce happier, of giving her a spiritual gift, I become happier as a result. I need to focus on giving to Joyce to balance my tendency toward self-centeredness. Joyce, on the other hand, has been learning to be fully true to her own heart. Whenever she does this, her devotion to me actually increases, because she is balancing the tendency of her early years to be overly devoted to me and not enough to herself.

God, the universal spirit of love, is just as much inside as outside us. Neither place is more or less important. Our highest commitment is to this spirit of love, rather than to a personality, whether it be our own or that of our beloved. Knowing and trusting this, our "sphere of commitment" will always remain balanced.

DIFFERENT DREAMS

It often happens that one partner in a relationship will feel called in a direction that challenges the other partner. When this happens, it is possible for the couple to remain united, even though their paths seem divergent.

We are each unique beings. So why expect that joining as a couple should somehow eliminate our individual dreams, visions, hopes—our individual paths to wholeness? Our ultimate destination is love, but the paths to that destination may differ as widely as we differ from each other.

Yet, for a relationship to work, there has to be a commitment to some fundamental baseline or ideal. There has to be a common ground from which each individual can branch out. The roots of the relationship have to be merged in the same soil, providing a solid base for the individuals to balance their own individual dreams with their shared dreams. Two lovers can have widely different personalities, philosophies, modes of expression, and interests, yet for their relationship to be fulfilling, they need to agree on the deepest level. Fulfilled couples share a *spiritual* common ground. For example, they agree that love is the most important ingredient for spiritual growth. Fulfilled couples also share a *relationship* common ground. For example, they agree that their relationship is more important than material or occupational status.

Each one of us has our own dreams. We need to continue dreaming in order to grow and thrive. Yet there are relationship-enhancing as well as relationship-damaging dreams. Relationship-enhancing dreams stretch the relationship in new directions, adding more growth, and deepening the couple's heart connection. The partner with these new dreams is thoughtful and considerate of their beloved. On the contrary, relationship-damaging dreams undermine the very foundation of the relationship. The partner wanting to pursue these new paths is usually self-preoccupied, not considerate of their lover's thoughts and feelings.

When I was a resident in psychiatry, I glimpsed the vision of Joyce and me leading groups of adults. Joyce's focus at the time was working with children, and when I shared my dream with her, she expressed her fear of being in front of groups of adults, her fear of feeling incompetent and being judged. I felt strong enough about this dream of our working together that I could simply love her and be present with her fears, understanding them rather than reacting to them and trying to change her feelings or, even worse, thinking she was standing in the way of my dream.

This is another key to how the mirror of relationship works. *When we cannot accept a quality or feeling in another, or when we struggle to change this person, these are clues that we are avoiding the mirror.* Feelings of aversion, dislike, or lack of acceptance indicate that we are projecting something that is ours onto another. On the other hand, *accepting the other person as they are, and feeling love and compassion for them, is truly seeing that person, more than merely seeing our own reflection.* In addition, feeling compassion for another person's struggle shows us our compassion for our own struggles. This positive reflection is also the mirror at work and an expression of our own spiritual growth and maturity.

The moment Joyce shared her fear with me, her fear became more important than my attachment to my dream. My dream was still important, and I trusted that we would someday work with groups of adults, but Joyce's feelings needed to be accepted and acknowledged first. As I did this, and Joyce felt no pressure from me to be different than she was, she felt an inner rightness about my dream. As her fear was recognized and accepted by me, she was able to recognize and accept her own fear and to begin the process of overcoming it. She now loves to work with groups of adults just as much as I do.

Then there are the relationship-damaging dreams. A number of years ago, I had an infatuation with a certain "spiritual teacher." I was convinced at the time that this person was "it" for me, but I let myself become unbalanced. I went a bit overboard, losing my center. (How often we are blind to when we are becoming unbalanced—when we are doing something that is affecting us—and our relationship—in an unhealthy way!)

This "teacher" was convinced Joyce and I were too intertwined with one another, too dependent on each other. She kept urging me to be more independent, not to hold hands so much, not to meditate together. To top it off, she felt Joyce's and my sexual relationship was preventing our growth into wholeness. She advocated abstinence, as well as sleeping in separate beds.

In my blinding zeal for spiritual evolution, I was accepting her "teaching." Joyce, meanwhile, felt pain and heaviness in her heart. There I was, seemingly excited about my "spiritual path," and it just didn't feel right to Joyce—it didn't ring true in her heart. Her doubting mind tried to tell her she was standing in the way of my good. When she would express these doubts to me, I felt she was trying to hold me back because of her own fear. Yet all the while, we both felt the painful lack of loving expression in our own relationship. This always has been, and always will be, an indicator that something is wrong. Some people tolerate a lack of love in their relationship more than others. Joyce and I find it difficult to ignore an impasse, and for this we've grown to be grateful.

Joyce finally had to accept it was not in her heart to support me in following this new path. So, trying to stay in the highest level of honesty, she expressed the pain she felt in connection with my actions. This was a key: *My actions were not the cause of the pain she felt.* My actions triggered her own feelings, feelings she was needing to work on in herself. Previously, she might have simply projected all of her own feelings onto me and gotten angry at me for "causing" her pain. Now, however, she could accept her responsibility to be honest with her pain without blaming me. She shared how much she missed me, and shared her longing and need for my love—*and physical affection.*

I was now faced with a big decision. Was this new path following my true dream or not? Was I listening to the desire of my heart, my real self? For most of us, this is not an easy decision, especially when one partner's "dream" coincides with another partner's suffering. It is possible for one partner to be following their heart and for that to threaten or scare the other partner but, with love and acceptance of the threatened partner's fears, the highest truth about the new dream is more easily revealed. If I was truly following my heart, it would bring peace and clarity to me, *and* more love and acceptance of my partner and all of her feelings.

Joyce's taking responsibility for her own feelings gave me the gift of more easily accessing my own true feelings. It took some deep soul-searching, but I finally saw the unhealthiness of this path I was on. I realized that it wasn't only separating us in our relationship, it was also separating me from my true inner self. Letting go of my new-found "path" was a humbling victory for me, yet a time of joyful celebration in our relationship.

In this case, our relationship was being threatened by the loss of our common ground, which was (and is) for us a commitment to follow our hearts, to love, and to believe that intimacy and closeness to one lover is a healthy choice.

If we want a fulfilling relationship, we need to honor one another's uniqueness—*and* find a spiritual and relationship common ground of love. We need to let our beloved follow their own heart, giving them the freedom to listen to their own inner direction. If that direction brings up feelings within us, we must take responsibility for these feelings, which might include sharing them. If we have cultivated a strong foundation of trust and respect, we will be able to bring a deeper peace into the relationship.

COMING BACK TOGETHER

Most couples spend many hours each day immersed in very different activities. Often one or both partners race out of the house each morning to drive to their separate workplaces. At the end of the day, they come back together and wonder why there is not more joy in their reunion.

When our first daughter, Rami, was a baby, I worked as a doctor in a general medical clinic in Santa Clara, an hour's drive from our home. Although I only worked two or three days a week, each shift was thirteen hours long, and involved my seeing a minimum of four patients an hour. Joyce, meanwhile, spent her day with all the duties of caring for a baby and keeping the house clean. Most days, she never saw another adult until I came home. The content of our days, to say the least, was quite different.

I would finally arrive home with a strange mixture of fatigue, nervous energy, and a mind cluttered with a whole collection of patients I had seen. Joyce was often fatigued also, but would be in a delicate and sensitive condition from nursing a newborn. No matter how gently I tried to enter the house, to her it would feel like the proverbial bull in a china shop. She would often feel jarred by my discordant energies and then pull back. I would sometimes feel hurt and rejected by her withdrawal. If only I could have understood in those moments that Joyce was my soul mirror, I could have seen her withdrawal from me as a reflection of my own jumbled state of mind.

We finally understood the need for a re-entry ritual. I needed to prepare spiritually for coming home. I did that by stopping for a walk in nature, listening to more gentle, meditative music while driving, and finally, sitting in the car for a short time before entering the house. During that time, I worked extra hard to calm down, to cleanse myself of the nervous energy I was bringing home. I found that the practice of visualizing light around myself (a practice used by many people in meditation) served as a way to quiet my mind. This helped me to come home to Joyce less nervous, less frenzied, and with my mind less filled with the troubled voices I had encountered during the day.

Joyce also needed to prepare herself for our reunion. Her favorite method was to remember that it was her beloved who was inside the sometimes busy and fatigued package that arrived home from a hectic day at work. Doing the same for Joyce was important for me too. Our inner work on our relationship was to see past each other's outer condition and hold firm to the real self, our true beloved beneath the surface. This was our spiritual relationship work, periodically to see each other (and ourselves), throughout the day, as our highest selves.

This combination of our joined effort helped immensely. Re-entry became a conscious process. Joy returned to our reunion.

Painful re-entry is not limited to couples. It includes parent-child reunions, friends getting together at the end of the day, and even dates. Bathing, grooming, and makeup are fine, but we also need to prepare ourselves in a deeper way to reunite with others. Meditation, breathing exercises, working with images of light, and concentrating on one another's inner beauty can allow for a more graceful and loving reconnection. It also helps to know the time as nearly as possible that a loved one will be arriving so we can begin to prepare for it. It may not seem like much, but it can make a huge difference when a working partner calls his or her partner at home and gives an updated arrival time.

When both partners cooperate in the re-entry process, there will be much more richness in the relationship. This is another reminder of the importance of inner work in relationship, especially the importance of seeing past the outer appearance of another person. When we take the time to remember who we are and who this other person is, that we are much greater than we appear, all of life takes on this greatness.

THE MIRROR ON THE PEDESTAL

Most of this chapter has focused on "negative" projections, qualities we don't like in another that are reflections of qualities we don't like in ourselves. However, positive projections, the goodness in ourselves that we can only see in another, can just as much stand in the way of relationship growth. When we see more beauty or strength in another than we do in ourselves, we do not feel equal to that person. We put them onto a pedestal and thus cannot have closeness. When we understand relationship as a mirror, we can realize the beauty we have projected onto this person is also within ourselves. Such a realization can restore equality to the relationship, and spiritual balance within ourselves.

John, a man in his early thirties, was convinced his wife of four years, Linda, was more spiritually evolved than himself. This conviction kept him from trying to be with her in a spiritual way, so he avoided praying or meditating with her, reading spiritual books with her, or discussing spiritual matters with her. Because he lifted her onto a pedestal, high above himself, he saw her as out of reach, and they couldn't have a close relationship.

Barry's and my work with John was to help him see that he was looking not only at Linda but also at a mirror reflection of himself. I encouraged him to look at, feel, and reclaim his own spiritual beauty. It was new for him to do this, because he had never thought of himself as a spiritual person. Yet it was also refreshing and eye-opening. As he realized Linda was not above or ahead of him, she became more of a real person, within relationship range.

Another example of an unhealthy "positive" projection took place in our own early relationship. In 1972, when Barry was a psychiatry resident, I worked in the department of child psychiatry at the University of Oregon Medical Center. Since the adult and child psychiatry departments were near each other, I always knew where Barry was. Whenever he was leading a group, it was easy for me to slip into the observation room to watch him through the window that was a mirror to him and the group. Usually, Barry's teachers and fellow residents were also in the little room for the purpose of critiquing his effectiveness with the group. I ignored their comments and concentrated all my attention upon Barry. More than simply being effective, I thought he was brilliant and compassionate.

One day, one of the psychiatrists noticed my joy-filled observation. She leaned close to me and whispered, "You could do just as good a job as Barry is doing right now."

I quickly responded, "Oh no, no. He has the gift. I could never do anything like that."

She smiled and said, "Look inside yourself."

Her last words impacted me deeply. I had always assumed Barry was better than me when it came to leading groups. I also felt he had better social skills. He was more outgoing and spoke freely with everyone. It seemed that people liked him more than me.

These "positive" projections were standing in the way of my feeling my own abilities and strengths. Gradually, the words of the psychiatrist began to sink in. All this time, I thought I was looking *through* the mirror of the observation room, when in fact I was looking *into* the mirror. I realized a powerful truth: *What we see in another, we already have in ourselves.* It wasn't wrong to see so much greatness in Barry. It was wrong not to see the greatness in myself. Seeing Barry as having something I didn't have was putting him on a pedestal above me and, therefore, preventing us from true closeness.

In the years that followed, with the help of friends and teachers, I grew in awareness of my own beauty and lovability. Rather than ceasing to see and appreciate the gifts of my beloved husband, because of my acceptance of my own gifts, I could see his even more clearly. Through reclaiming what I saw in the mirror of my relationship, I grew in self-acceptance and self-confidence and allowed a deeper closeness in our relationship.

Barry and I now enjoy leading groups together, which brings a deep fulfillment to both of us. Recognizing my own strengths has allowed my leadership to be rewarding, purposeful, and fun.

RECLAIMING YOUR PROJECTIONS

Now it's up to you. You have the courage to look into the mirror of relationship and see what you may have blindly projected there. The negativity you see in another is loudly telling you something about your own negativity in that moment. The differences you have trouble accepting in another are reflecting back those things you have trouble accepting in yourself. And, just as importantly, the beauty and strength you behold in another is not just *out there*. It's in you, too. It takes courage to acknowledge that you are what you see—that how you are feeling in any particular moment will be instantaneously reflected by how the world and everyone in it appears to you. Exercise this courage—look deeply into the mirror of life—and live life to the fullest potential!

12

Anger in the Mirror

For one human being to love another, that is the most difficult of all our tasks, the ultimate, the last test and proof, the work for which all other work is but preparation.

—RAINER MARIA RILKE

OWHERE IS THE CONCEPT OF "SOUL MIRRORS" more useful than in dealing with anger, that fiery emotion that can wreak such havoc in relationships. When we're angry at someone close to us, we usually don't want to see them as a mirror of ourselves. That is, we don't want to accept that our anger is actually telling us something about ourselves, reflecting back to us the qualities in ourselves we are not accepting. However, if we want to grow in love and friendship, we need to take responsibility for our angry feelings. We need to understand the process of projection, that we unconsciously take the unacceptable parts of ourselves and attribute them to another. Projection can be extremely subtle, making it difficult for us to see that it's ourselves we're not loving when we're angry, not our partner.

Don shared with Joyce and me one day in our office, "I'm so angry at my mother-in-law. She criticizes me ruthlessly for so many of the decisions I've made concerning the family. How I would love her parental acceptance!"

I asked him, "How do *you* feel about those decisions you've made?"

Don shot back without thinking, "I feel fine about them."

Yet after a moment's silence, he more humbly added, "I take that back. I'm not so sure they were the best decisions."

I told him, "That's why you get so angry at your mother-in-law. If you were at peace with your decisions, you wouldn't get angry. You might feel sad about her criticizing you, but the anger is showing your inner criticism of yourself."

Don's mother-in-law was a mirror for him. Her criticism of him was reflecting his own criticism of himself.

Likewise, when someone is angry at us, it is often hard to see how they are, at least in part, projecting onto us their own frustration and their anger at themselves. Armed with this awareness, however, we will be in a better position to accept another person's anger as well as our own.

Anger happens. We may wish it didn't. We may wish we could get to a point in our relationships where we wouldn't need to ever get angry, but as long as we have these bodies, we are immersed in the human condition. And that includes experiencing anger. Yet anger does not have to be a scourge. In fact, we are blessed when we open ourselves to the lessons anger has to teach us.

First, it's important to understand the nature of anger, as well as its purpose and usefulness. Anger is a form and use of energy, a way our energy or vitality is put into action. Most often, it is a way we protect ourselves from the rawness of pain or fear—feelings that can become unbearable to our sometimes fragile and naked psyches.

Many people share that anger is the hardest part of their relationship and often ask us for constructive ways to work with anger when it comes up. First, we need to distinguish between anger and ANGER. There is a big difference between the little annoyances that are inevitable in relating and the more serious anger that arises from deeper issues. It may not be appropriate to look for deeper meaning in the common annoyances. We may simply need to pay closer attention to our habit patterns. If something we do annoys our partner, we need to ask ourselves how important it is for us to continue this behavior. Perhaps it's something we can let go of for the sake of harmony.

In addition, we need to be willing to resolve these little frustrations, to see them through to the end, to apologize sincerely when it is clear that something we did upset our partner. It is just as important to communicate our own upset at something our partner did or said. And it is always best to have these communications in the moment, rather than waiting for a better time. Otherwise, these little upsets become buried in the soil of our being, only to explode out of us later. Also, if you wait to voice your annoyance until the sixth time your partner does that certain irritating thing, it's only the first time your partner has heard your feelings. It may (or may not) take five more practice times before they remember to quit.

When anger reaches a certain level of intensity, we need to understand that deeper issues may be crying out for attention. This higher amplitude of anger more often relates back to hurts older than the relationship, but is triggered by the present situation. For example, Harold, during a workshop, was angry at his wife because she left to go to the bathroom without telling him. His reaction was simply out of proportion to the offense. On deeper questioning, he shared that he felt abandoned by his wife. When asked if he had felt abandoned by anyone else, he revealed a profound abandonment by his mother, who left him when he was six years old. For Harold, his wife's action triggered the same feelings caused by his mother's abandonment.

Anger is not only an attack, it is most often a defense against hurt. It's difficult not to take it personally when our partner gets angry at us, because it usually feels like we are being attacked or blamed. But this is the smoke screen. The yelling or fuming is actually just a way the person is covering up their hurt or pain. It's a sign that they are hurting. It is essential to remember this.

Anger, therefore, is a cry for help. One of the highest things Joyce and I do in our own relationship is to recognize this truth. When one of us gets angry, the other tries to remember this is a call for help and tries to listen as openly as possible. When we're angry, we long for acceptance of our feelings. Joyce has told me she needs me to hold her when she is upset, even though it appears she is attacking me. This is not easy for me and requires some of the deepest courage I can muster. In fact, I can give support to angry strangers and friends far more easily than I can to Joyce. With Joyce, because of my attachment to her, I tend to immediately react to her anger at me as a personal offense. Still, I have on a few occasions immediately reached out and held her in my arms even though she was angry at me. This has helped her to let go of the anger and access the pain underneath. Other times, Joyce has been able to reach through my anger at her and hold me. We each need this connection just as much. Often, we are not successful at this method in the early stages of anger and get locked into defensiveness, which escalates the anger.

Remembering that anger is a call for help allows us to be defenseless, and ironically, in defenselessness lies our real strength. When we forget that anger is a call for help, we instead feel attacked and become defensive in an effort to protect ourselves. But as we more and more understand that someone who is angry is someone who is hurting, we can respond with more love. The proverbial lion with the thorn in its paw roars with pain and rage. You could feel defensive and assume the lion is angry at you. After all, this wild beast is loudly roaring and facing your direction. Or you could understand the roaring has nothing to do with you. The animal is simply in pain, and you can gently reassure it while you remove the thorn.

Any buildup of energy needs to be released, vented, or transformed in some way. Anger is no different. Sometimes it just needs to be expressed as a release of steam, and we then feel better—and can perhaps subsequently access our deeper feelings of hurt or fear. What we must remember, however, is that anger does not need to be directed at our partner to be released. It can be effectively expressed by ourselves, for example, by yelling or beating on pillows. It is important that we not ignore or distract ourselves from this energy. Sometimes, simply expressing anger in self-describing words ("I'm feeling angry right now") is helpful. Other times, it doesn't need to be expressed outwardly. It can be enough to feel (and accept that you feel) angry as another way to accept your humanity. Writing in your journal can be a helpful tool, as can physical exercise or being out in nature.

Ultimately, if we want to grow spiritually, we need to take full responsibility for our anger and what is behind it. It is up to each one of us to accept and confront the hurt, pain, or fear hiding underneath our anger. To maintain an angry stance is self-defeating, because it continues to cloak our deeper, more vulnerable, feelings.

The most destructive thing about our anger is not how it hurts others, although it can hurt others terribly. The most damage caused by anger is what is does to ourselves. Our anger will always hurt us more than the person we may be trying to hurt. Angry feelings rob us of our peace and our vitality and can literally make us sick. Even deeper, maintaining anger hurts us most because it keeps us from learning the lessons we need to learn in our lives. For example, our anger may be trying to teach us about our unrealistic expectations, such as how we want to change another person rather than let them be who they are.

One of the ways we can prevent angry feelings is by taking better care of ourselves. Anger is most often a cry for help from within. Our inner child needs love and acceptance from ourselves most of all. When we forget this and try to get it from our partner or from anyone else, we can become frustrated, disappointed—and angry.

DIFFERENT STYLES OF ANGER

Couples often ask us for help bringing into harmony their own particular styles of expressing anger. We have found that each couple has a unique pattern during periods of disharmony, and what works for one couple doesn't necessarily work for another. There are, however, some fairly common styles. It is important that we recognize our styles of expressing anger. Only then can we accept ourselves and our partner, and change the behaviors in ourselves we want to change.

Often one person is more a "venter," while the other is more a "smolderer." This tends to be our own pattern. Joyce's anger flares up immediately like a flame, then relatively quickly burns itself out. Mine tends to be more like smoldering coals, not as hot as a flame but longer lasting. You can see, therefore, that Joyce will typically be ready to reconcile before I am. However, this is never a black-and-white situation. Styles of anger, like styles of living in general, can change from situation to situation. Sometimes I vent and Joyce smolders, and then I am the first one ready to reestablish harmony.

Joyce grew up in a family where anger was usually held in and therefore expressed through tense silence. My family, on the other hand, was loud. Their voices were loud; their anger was loud. Everything was not only expressed—it was overexpressed! We feel that perhaps our own styles of anger are reactive patterns to the climate in our childhood homes, which we each learned from the modeling by our families. However, we have also seen other couples where the pattern is not reactive. Their styles of anger seem to have been learned and then internalized from their family upbringing. In any case, our patterns are our patterns. They may be much deeper than family upbringing.

Another typical pattern in couples is the "push-run" syndrome. When there is disharmony, and therefore insecurity, one partner "pushes" for communication and resolution of the disharmony, while the other partner "runs" away either physically or emotionally. Joyce and I used to have this tendency early in our relationship. She would push for communication because she found the lack of love between us intolerable. I ran away because I felt so vulnerably raw and unprotected, and also because it took me longer to sort out my feelings (remember, I'm the smolderer). Joyce would then react with fear at being abandoned, physically as well as emotionally, and would push even more for communication and connection. I would react to feeling pressured and would run even further away. It was not a very productive cycle!

Thank God we didn't stay long in this whirlpool of energy. We would remember we are safe—not just safe with each other, but safe in the arms of *love itself*. We would remember that the other person was not deliberately trying to hurt or abandon us. This gave us the courage to take the first steps toward reconciliation.

If you consider your relationship a sacred thing, you will naturally want to do whatever it takes to heal the unhealthy patterns in your lives. And what a blessed opportunity that is! Respect is a key word. We need to learn how to respect each other's differences. We need to learn how to accept our partner just the way they are, rather than trying to make them be more like us. It is their difference which brings diversity, balance and, yes, even more beauty into our lives.

UNDERSTANDING YOUR ANGER PATTERN

Ponder the following questions:

What is your style of anger expression?

What is your partner's style of anger expression?

How is each style helpful?

How is each style self-defeating?

What were your family patterns while you were growing up?

Set aside a time to talk with one another about your styles of anger. Please do not point out your partner's pattern unless he or she sincerely asks for your help. It is always safer to try to be vulnerable and talk about your own patterns and struggles.

THE BLAME PLAN

As young, rather immature freshmen in college, Barry and I each had a strongly developed sense of stubborn self-righteousness. I remember a walk we took when we were eighteen. We were having a pleasant time being together until we started discussing which side of the road we should walk on. The discussion escalated into an argument. We ended up each walking on a different side of the road, glaring at each other the whole way. A friend walked by in the middle of the road and asked what was going on. We were embarrassed as we tried to explain that the other wouldn't walk on "our" side. The friend shook his head in dismay at our stubbornness and walked on. We felt rather foolish, but we continued on our own sides of the road.

Our early years were like a giant roller coaster ride—deep closeness and passionate attraction alternating with stubborn defiance that caused us to act in the most ridiculous ways. I can now smile at our early displays of anger. The first time I was really angry at Barry, I kicked him in his shin. He kicked me back. This started a physical confrontation that was observed by a bunch of dorm students who happened to be looking out their window. Everyone assumed our relationship was hopeless. At the end of our sophomore year, our classmates voted *us* the couple least likely to succeed.

We have progressed and are more mature in our expressions of anger. I don't kick Barry anymore, nor do we hurt each other physically. The stubbornness, however, is very much alive and well. Both of us rebel strongly whenever we feel dominated.

People are sometimes surprised that the authors of many books on relationships could have just as much anger as anyone else. We feel it is this very humanness that gives us the power to write and teach about this subject that we grapple with passionately every day of our lives.

Several years ago, Barry and I were having a particularly difficult time in our relationship. We had just built our house, which we were also using as a retreat center. The building phase went smoothly; we seemed to agree on most every decision. The stress came when we realized how high our mortgage payments were.

When we first married, we decided we never wanted money to be an issue. We maintained a simple lifestyle, drove old cars, bought our clothes from thrift shops, and managed to avoid owning a credit card. For twenty years, we refused to owe money for anything.

The earthquake changed all that. We were forced out of our inexpensive rental home into the world of high-priced rentals. We decided to go for our dream of owning land and building, but we had no idea our mortgage would climb so high. We began to feel insecure, and, for the first time in our marriage, money became an issue. The stress and uncertainty weighed heavily on us, and we began arguing more than ever before.

Fortunately after several months, we realized we could make the necessary financial adjustment. We started trusting that our financial needs would be met just as all our needs have always been met.

Until we made this shift into trusting, we projected our own stress and insecurity onto each other and blamed each other. We were ignoring the mirror of relationship, refusing to see how the real pain was coming from within. We both realized this projection needed to be confronted and was showing itself more frequently so we could seriously look at it. We started spending more time together to look at our relationship and the old stuck patterns of relating. Just when we would think we were clear in our understanding, the old habit of anger, blame, and stubbornness would assert itself again. When that energy was present between us, our times of clarity and understanding seemed far away.

One day our anger was on the rise, and we were loudly and stubbornly blaming each other. Our daughters, Rami and Mira, came upon us and were upset at seeing their parents so locked into mutual blame. We usually try our hardest to shield our children from our arguments. Sometimes we will go into another room. Sometimes we'll wait until they leave. Once in a while, it does happen that the children witness our conflict. We feel that they sometimes need to see our disharmony—as well as witness how we work through each argument. In these times, we are giving our children a model of how two people can be angry with each other and eventually come back into harmony.

Rami, who was learning assertiveness in high school, told us we were acting like children and should see a counselor. Mira just watched us sadly. I looked at Rami. At age sixteen she was as wise and mature as any grown woman I knew, yet simple and childlike as well. Then I looked at Mira. At age eleven she was still so beautifully a child, full of trust and love.

Rami repeated her intervention, "Mom, Dad, stop acting like children! Why don't you get help?"

Barry and I looked at each other and sat down. The girls sat near us. We knew Rami was right. We did need some help. We considered who we might go to. We wanted a person who could walk their talk, who was practicing what they were preaching. Then we started thinking about other qualities we would want in a counselor. It had to be someone who wouldn't take sides, who would see and respect each side equally. And it had to be someone who wouldn't be afraid to confront each of us on our issues.

While we were thinking about who we could see for help, Rami lit up like a beacon and said, "I can help you both."

We immediately agreed, so she took our hands and led us into her room. Mira followed and we all sat down. Rami then proceeded to give an accurate account of how she saw both sides. She had witnessed many arguments between us over the span of her lifetime, usually over small things, but all having a similar pattern of each of us wanting to be right, each blaming the other and each clinging to stubbornness. She was able to talk to both of us so we were able to better understand the other's point of view. After counseling couples for twenty years, it was humbling to have our sixteen-year-old daughter reflect to us such a clear picture of our stuck patterns.

Barry and I spent the rest of the day together, while the girls watched John-Nuriel for us. We realized we had come to a point in our growth where we had no choice but to give up blaming each other for issues in our relationship. We could go no longer seeing the other at fault. It was time to take full responsibility ourselves for stepping out of love, for closing our hearts.

This realization came powerfully, and we knew we needed a plan to fulfill it. We saw that as we dropped blame and self-righteousness, our relationship was going to soar to greater heights. We glimpsed the blessing of this change and developed a plan that we could put into action whenever this negative pattern threatened to assert itself.

We offer our plan to you as a model that you will need to customize, for each relationship is different and so are the negative patterns. We hope you'll be challenged in your relationship to uncover these patterns and develop a plan to help you rise above them. The plan you develop will not only help your relationship, but also your individual growth. Whenever you challenge yourself to overcome a dynamic that does not serve you, love and strength come to fill the void.

In the past, as Barry has described, whenever I would start to feel even the slightest distancing between Barry and me, I would start talking about it immediately. I would urgently look for reasons for our disharmony (and, forgetting the mirror, in my mind Barry was usually at fault). Barry would often feel attacked and blamed by my words and would then, in turn, blame me. With my anger in his face, Barry would feel desperate for space and would tend to leave. That made me feel even worse. Eventually, he started experimenting with staying and yelling back. We were still blaming each other, but at least we were *both* getting the anger out.

So, we agreed that at any point in this process of anger and blame, either one of us could call the following "plan" into action. Both of us are equally committed to carrying it out. Both of us had just as much input in its creation.

First we agree to sit together silently for five minutes with our eyes closed. During this time, we are to focus on how we ourselves *stepped out of love.* The point here is to focus on our own mistakes rather than the other's. This part is harder for me than for Barry, but knowing it will only be five minutes makes it more tolerable.

After five minutes, we open our eyes and verbally appreciate each other. Now, this is hard to do, even more so for Barry than for me. When I'm feeling distant from Barry, the last thing I want to do is appreciate him, but the very act of looking for something positive

changes the negative feeling. It may be difficult to start, but appreciating each other aloud is a method that has always helped us in the
past.

The first appreciations might be superficial:

"Thank you for packing special lunches for the children this
morning."

"I appreciate how you took the garbage out without my having to
ask you."

If we keep at it, we allow the appreciations to deepen:

"I appreciate how much love you have given me all these years."

"I appreciate that you are willing to work out these difficulties
with me so we can begin to feel close again."

After we have appreciated each other in meaningful ways, we are
then ready for the next part. We each share how we believe we alone
stepped out of love. We say as clearly as possible what we ourselves did
to contribute to the disharmony. Once we each take personal responsibility for our part of the fight, the fight is over. There is nothing
more to fight about. The deeper issue behind the anger and blame
can now be focused on for healing.

When we were arguing about money, for example, the real issue,
seen in the light of the mirror, was our own insecurity. Projecting this
insecurity onto each other, we each perceived a lack of trust coming
from the other person, got angry, and blamed each other. Yet as we
each accepted responsibility for our own insecurity about money, we
could share this with each other, allow ourselves to become more vulnerable, and comfort one another. With this new awareness—and a
few months experience of seeing all the bills get paid—we gained a
renewed faith and trust that our finances would always work out.

Our plan has served us beautifully each time we have used it.
However, there are times when we rebel, feel too hurt, or just want to
indulge in our old blame habit. Each time this happens, we once again
ultimately see how destructive blame is to our harmony and union.
We hope that, through the use of our plan, we will eventually train
our minds automatically to recognize our own mistakes rather than
blame each other. We are striving to change and grow ourselves,

rather than trying to change one another. Since we have made and used our plan, we have come into even closer love and respect as a couple.

THE PLAN IN ACTION

On a recent river trip, Joyce, the kids, and I were looking forward to a special hike up a side stream to a magical waterfall. John-Nuriel was excited to prove his capability to do this hike. With his sisters just ahead of him, we all set off.

Five minutes into the hike, with the girls and our friends just ahead of us and out of sight, John-Nuri started to get upset at being behind. I *assumed* Joyce heard his complaining and saw his upset. Wrong assumption! At that moment, Joyce remembered John-Nuri's life jacket. She thought he would need it upstream at a place where we needed to swim through a deep pool with cliffs on both sides. She asked me to run back and get the life jacket while the two of them waited. She felt afraid of the several stream crossings without my help. John-Nuri was clearly agitated, because now he couldn't see or hear the others, but for whatever reason, Joyce did not know this.

I told Joyce it would take too much time to get the life jacket, and also I felt we didn't need it anyway. I felt confident of my ability to swim through the pool with John-Nuri.

Not knowing how important it was for John-Nuri to catch up, Joyce assumed I was just being lazy. The life jacket was important to her. She was thinking about John-Nuri's safety. I was thinking about his happiness. Both of us were trying to be the best parents we could.

For Joyce, the situation also brought up another issue. In the past, I had not always been as sensitive as Joyce to John-Nuri's needs. It had been a cause of friction, especially on the river trips, because Joyce felt less physically confident. This kind of "button-pushing" concerning issues from the past is often a cause of arguments rapidly escalating.

With lightning speed, the disagreement escalated into anger, blame, yelling, even name-calling. Joyce left me with John-Nuri while she went back to get the life jacket. I went ahead with him to try to catch up. When Joyce finally did catch up to us both, there was even more anger than before. With the added elements of emotional wounding and the feeling of betrayal, it was the adults who were needing a life jacket!

It wasn't until hours later that we were finally ready to sit with each other and put our "plan" into action. The pain of not being in harmony is too much for us to endure for long. It is often that very suffering that urges us to look within and take responsibility for our own part of the argument. So, when we sat with each other, we had both had enough sadness and were both ready to look inside.

For my part, I realized my wrong assumption about Joyce's awareness of John-Nuri's feelings. Joyce realized her wrong assumption about me being lazy. We were able to appreciate one another as good, caring parents. We could each apologize for the unkind words that had been spoken in anger. When we finally smiled and embraced, we heard a loud clapping and cheering from our children and friends in the kitchen area of our campsite. Slightly embarrassed at our lack of privacy on this particular beach, we smiled and hugged even more at the joy of feeling close once again.

CREATING A BLAME PLAN

Now you need to come up with your own "blame plan." It may be with a partner, a parent, a child, or a close friend. Choose a time when you are feeling close to create your plan, rather than a time when you are feeling desperate for such a plan, as in the heat of an argument.

Feel what would most help you to move beyond blaming this person. Do you need a period of silence? Appreciation? Whatever it takes to show you how *you* "stepped out of love" or closed your heart. You may wish to follow our plan as a model or come up with one specifically designed for your own unique needs. Your plan must be unique to your own relationship. Make sure the plan is totally agreeable to both of you— ideally, both of you have input rather than one of you coming up with the plan.

Some people have discovered that prearranged hand gestures or other physical signals can be an important part of the plan, especially in the beginning when verbal communication has broken down. For example, making the letter T with your two hands, as in "Time out," might be a cue for a period of silence.

Share your plan with your friends. It will help you in your commitment to your own plan, and it may help them.

ONE-SIDED BLAME

An especially dangerous form of blame is one-sided blame, where one partner blames the other for a certain problem and the "blamed" partner agrees. This is a conspiracy that will steadily work to destroy the relationship—*and* block the growth of the individuals involved.

To blame another is to miss out on the goodness in both of you. In order for you to blame someone, you must close your heart to them, stopping the feeling of love. It's not possible to close your heart to another and still keep it open to your own goodness. Likewise, to accept the blame from another is to close your heart to your own beauty and goodness. And closing your heart to yourself stops the flow of love to both of you. Both of you, therefore, lose no matter which direction the blame is flowing.

In a recent workshop, Larry revealed a problem he was having in his twenty-year marriage. Not only had he had an affair with another woman, but he had fallen in love with her as well. As Larry spoke, he hung his head in shame, and while tears flowed, he shared the pain this had brought to his wife and children. Cynthia, his wife, sat next to him with a distant, unchanging expression. It appeared her heart was closed to her husband.

As they talked, it was clear they both blamed Larry as the cause of this crisis in their marriage. This feeling of blame was going to keep them from ever feeling close to one another. Larry wanted desperately to be forgiven by Cynthia, yet could not forgive himself since he was feeling himself deeply at fault. Cynthia felt innocent and righteously indignant at Larry's betrayal of their twenty-year commitment.

As I sat watching this couple, I was drawn back to 1971 when Barry and I had been married three years. We had been in love with each other for seven years, and I thought we had a great relationship. We were attracted to one another, and the energy that flowed between us was alive and enthusiastic. I felt totally devoted to Barry. I was supporting him financially through medical school, a task my women's liberation friends complained about, yet which I considered an honor. I cooked, cleaned, and took care of all the earthly details for him so he could study, even though I had a full-time job as a nurse. I met him every day for lunch, a time in which we kissed and hugged a lot.

Then Barry had the "affair." I felt totally betrayed, and my only thought was to leave our relationship completely, which, as I explained earlier, I did. Over the course of the next week, Barry went through quite a profound healing and growth change. We got back together, but something was missing—something had died in our relationship. We continued to meet for lunch every day, but the kissing and hugging lacked the spontaneity they had before. The wound from the affair was still fresh and seemed to create distance between us. I felt Barry had acted wrongly, that *he* was the cause of the distance and pain we both felt. Barry also felt at fault, feeling that if it weren't for *his* mistake, we could have continued the early marital bliss we had been enjoying.

Had we stayed in that pattern of one-sided blame, our marriage would probably not have survived. Fortunately, a good friend saw that we were at an impasse and suggested I start looking at the ways I had contributed to Barry's affair. At first, I was incredulous. *Me* take any responsibility for this problem? I had been the model wife.

Yet as the days and weeks went by, I examined my own behavior. I had always been overly focused on Barry, believing he needed excessive attention and care from me. I began to understand that in my exuberant devotion to him, I had been neglecting myself. *I was respecting who he was more than who I was.* This was my model of a good wife. I was concentrating more on *his* beauty and strengths than my own. And partly because of this, Barry was respecting me a little less as well. Neither of us was aware of the unhealthiness of my one-sided devotion.

I began to turn my total devotion to husband into devotion to the God-self, the higher consciousness, within us both. I began to honor my own beauty, strengths, and abilities. As I became a more whole person within myself, Barry was able to love and respect me more deeply. Because I had never really shown my strength in saying "No" to Barry, he assumed I would continue being devoted no matter what he did. We both began to see that the affair was not just Barry's fault, but the outgrowth of an unhealthy pattern in our marriage, an excessively one-sided devotion that was not serving either of us.

I no longer felt totally innocent; Barry no longer took all the blame. With that change of perspective, we joined on a deeper level than ever before. Now there was even more respect and appreciation and a renewed commitment in our marriage. We again chose a path of monogamy, but now with more understanding. Our kissing and hugging during lunch took on a deeper feeling than ever before. Twenty-three years later, we still look back upon that time as the real beginning of our spiritual marriage to each other, to our becoming mirrors of one another's souls.

Carol and Len's story offers another view of one-sided blame: Len was adamant that Carol spent too much of their money. Some of it was spent on herself, on clothes, jewelry. A good portion of it, however, was spent on personal and relationship growth, such as workshops, self-help books and tapes, bodywork, and therapy. When he would criticize her for this, she would feel ashamed and guilty, even though he was benefiting from those growth tools.

Yet they were both only seeing part of the picture. Although Carol spent more money than Len, she also gave more love and nurturing to Len than he did to her. Likewise, Len spent less money and also tended to withhold his love—the currency of the heart. With the help of therapy, Carol began to see how the unhealthy part of her spending increased whenever she felt criticized or blamed by Len, especially when she felt guilty and ashamed of herself and saw herself as having the bigger problem in the relationship. Len began to see the unhealthy aspects of his holding back, whether it be money or love. More important, they saw the ways they were each contributing to the problem equally, rather than one of them more than the other.

Blaming your partner for a problem in your relationship will stifle love and eventually cause the relationship to die. We need to look within ourselves for the ways we contribute to the difficulties in our intimate relationships. Everything that happens in our relationships is an intricate dance in which both partners are involved. As we learn this, we will not only grow tremendously ourselves, but we will help free our beloved of guilt and shame, allowing him or her to grow as well. As hard as problems are, they afford us a tremendous chance to grow as a couple. As each partner is willing to look inside and grow, so also can the relationship spiral upward to greater love and intimacy.

UNCOVERING ONE-SIDED BLAME

Is there a conspiracy of unilateral blame in your relationship? Is there a problem in your relating that you attribute mostly to the other person? Or do you feel blamed by your partner or someone close to you and accept their blame, therefore feeling guilt or shame?

It is time to remember that relationship is a dance involving more than one person. What is the "innocent" person's part in the dance? How are they (or you) contributing to the unhealthiness of the relationship?

Take time to feel your answers to these questions. Then write your reflections down in a journal or diary and/or share them with a partner.

The Healing Power of Touch

Have you ever noticed that you can be feeling anger and distance from your partner and still have flashes of attraction for them? Usually the mind stifles the feeling of attraction or refuses to let it come to the surface: "I'm not attracted to you. I'm angry at you." However, the feeling of attraction and anger can be happening at the same time. When two people love each other and become angry, their bodies can still feel attraction. That is because our bodies are slower to register all the intricacies of our mental and emotional conflicts. Our bodies hold deep memories of closeness, cuddling, and warm feelings from the past. It is almost as if our bodies say to each other, "Who cares that your mind was forgetful or insensitive? Let's make up for it by snuggling and having warm good feelings again." The ego, on the other hand, does not work that way and insists upon proving its point and even getting revenge. The fact that our bodies, at least for awhile, still desire closeness can be a valuable key to ending conflict.

Scientists are beginning to understand how touch stimulates the release of endorphins, the body's mood-elevating chemicals. Caresses can actually reduce blood pressure and help people to feel more peaceful and calm. Often, while touching, we can more easily find the resolution of the conflict.

Several times a year, Barry and I offer workshops solely for couples. Usually we attract committed couples who want to deepen as well as heal their relationship. Sometimes a few couples will come who are in serious trouble. In one workshop, a couple came who felt ready to end their relationship. Evelyn and Wally were angry with each other and felt alienated. Both felt like giving up on their union. Their distance from one another became painfully obvious to them as we began the various workshop exercises. As couples stood in front of the group in the beginning to introduce one another, Wally and Evelyn stood quite separate and had difficulty expressing any positive words for each other. During a subsequent communication exercise, the atmosphere in the room was alive as the other couples were taking risks and sharing difficult areas of relating. Evelyn and Wally lay down in the back of the room, separate from each other, and dozed.

The evening of the workshop evolved into a discussion on conflict resolution. We shared how, if the two of us are not getting along when we go to sleep, we often lie close together and agree to talk more about the conflict in the morning. As our bodies lie together, we begin to relax, feel calmer inside, and eventually fall asleep together. In the morning, the resolution comes more quickly. If ours is a more serious conflict, we may not be able to go to sleep, but the physical closeness helps us to then sit up in bed and work things out.

That night, Wally and Evelyn went to a friend's house to sleep. This was to be their first time sleeping together in quite a while. Usually their young children needed them at night, so they each took turns sleeping with the children. This night, however, the children were with baby-sitters. Since communication between them was shut down, they decided to take our advice and merely lie close together in bed. They woke in the morning in each other's arms. That morning, Evelyn and Wally were able to communicate and begin resolving their differences. When they returned to the retreat, we could hardly believe the positive change in them. They realized an important part of their healing was simply allowing the time for physical closeness.

Snuggling, hugging, and touching each other (especially in a nonsexual way) is an essential ingredient for every relationship. Enough touching can be a wonderful preventive measure against the painful separation and conflict many couples endure. Such a simple act can carry much power to sustain and heal our relationships far beyond what the mind thinks possible.

EMBRACING YOUR ANGER

Prepare for quiet time or meditation.

Feel or imagine your angry feelings are like a red ball of fire in the area of your solar plexus (navel). Feel and/or visualize this red ball carefully.

Now, instead of trying to push it away or get rid of it, realize this red ball needs your acceptance. Place your hands around it. Notice it is not hot like ordinary fire. Rather, it is warm to the touch. Hold this warm ball like you would hold a small child needing your love and acceptance.

Notice as you do this, the ball is actually warming you from the inside, bringing more life energy into your being. As you embrace this red ball of fire, know that it is giving you a gift.

As you embrace your anger, accepting and acknowledging that you have these feelings, your anger embraces you. It becomes your friend, your ally, rather than your enemy.

13

The Importance of Saying "No"

To love truth is better than to know it.

—CONFUCIUS

LEARNING TO SAY "NO" *WHEN WE FEEL IT* IS A fundamental step in learning to love. It is good to say "Yes" as many times as possible, but that is only half of life's equation of balance. Learning to say an honest "No" to another person really means that we are first having a relationship with ourselves—honoring our feelings, respecting our boundaries, and loving ourselves. For many people, this is a difficult lesson to master.

Whenever a situation arises where there is a need to make a "Yes" or "No" decision, train yourself first to listen inside to feel if it is right for you. If you cannot access your inner feeling right away, then simply ask for more time to make the decision. It is critical to feel this rightness within yourself before you commit yourself to anything.

Abraham Lincoln, perhaps one of our finest presidents, is said to have taken a long time making decisions. He often did not consult a complex advisory board like modern-day presidents. Instead, he relied on his intuition. Sometimes it was frustrating to others to wait for him to feel the right decision. When he finally did receive the clear intuitive answer, he acted with great strength and conviction, without wavering or doubting his decision.

We have seen many relationships where one partner pressures the other into doing what they want. The pressured partner goes along because they feel it is easier to yield than to stand up for what they feel. In this situation, both partners lose. Partners that yield because of pressure respect themselves less, are likely to feel resentful, and are going against their own natural guidance. The partners who win really do not win at all, because they have won through pressure rather than through love and respect. By being allowed to win in this way, these partners lose respect both for themselves and for their bullied partner.

When our oldest daughter Rami was an infant, we lived in Mt. Shasta on retreat for the summer. The entire retreat was devoted to strengthening our ability to listen to our own inner voices. One day, Barry had gone off exploring and came back excited about a place he had found. It was a gorgeous little lake, ten miles up a bumpy, boulder-strewn jeep road. Barry wanted to take Rami and me camping there. I told him I needed to sit and see if it felt right to me.

As I sat alone, I immediately felt that I shouldn't take Rami there. Something about the proposed trip didn't feel good and I received a clear "No."

I went back and told Barry. His face drooped with disappointment as he said, "Oh, I want so much to show you this great place." I couldn't bear the disappointment my response had caused him, so I agreed to go.

Right away, I started to get a sick feeling in my stomach. I knew I was going against my inner feeling, but I wanted to please Barry. With each mile of the bumpy road, I felt worse. Sure enough, six miles into the wilderness, the clutch on our old VW van broke. It took the entire day and into the evening to drive our clutchless bus back home. Each mile seemed like an eternity. Rami cried just about the whole time. It was a miserable day for us all.

Through experiences like that, Barry and I are learning to honor and respect our own inner "No"s as well as the inner "No" of our partner. We are also learning to be grateful rather than disappointed or resentful when our partner doesn't feel good about a plan or idea. Loving someone involves accepting them right where they are, letting them have their feelings, and letting them say their "No"s. We've found through much trial and error that decisions and plans only work when we both feel good about them.

I remember a time when a "No" came to me in our relationship in a strong way. In 1972, when Barry was in his last year of medical school, I felt we were close. We spent as much time as possible together. However, we still had some unhealthy patterns in our marriage. Barry was pushing for deeper connections with other women, feeling that he needed this for his own growth. I was feeling insecure but unable to say "No." Barry's desire was bringing my own insecurity to the surface of my awareness. Our relationship was about to go through a huge test.

When a good friend of mine came to visit from across the continent, I recognized at once an attraction that had always existed between Barry and her. This attraction had been playful for them and tolerable to me. It had not been a problem. Their actions toward one another had always seemed appropriate for good friends, as well as respectful of me.

This time, however, she was coming to us in need. Her husband of one year was leaving her for another woman. We both felt a lot of compassion for our friend and wanted to comfort her. However, she seemed to be reaching out a little more to Barry than to me, which worried me.

The following day, I needed to work while Barry had a free day from school. I asked him to do something special with my friend. I hoped they would have a good time. I was not prepared that they would become sexual.

When Barry told me about their day, he sincerely wanted me to know that he loved me just as much as before. Rather than keeping their affair a dark secret, he was trying to be honest and open with me. He truly did not understand how much pain and violation his actions would cause me. Still, I was devastated. What I remember most clearly from the experience was the "NO!" that seemed to surge through my body in a deep and instinctual way. I knew without any doubt that I could not live with this. I locked myself in the bathroom and screamed and cried for hours.

At four in the morning, I was lying on the bathroom floor considering my options. I felt that I had only two choices. I could try to live with Barry's desire for openness with other women (and have no guarantee that it would not again cross the boundary into sexual openness), or I could honor the "No" inside me, take care of myself, and leave. Even in that moment of feeling enraged, I felt compassion for both of us. I loved Barry more than anyone in the world, yet I knew I must first honor myself. Looking into the mirror of my love for Barry, I could see a more essential love, a love of myself. To honor this love, I needed to leave the relationship.

Silently, I crept out of the bathroom, packed some clothes, called our dog, and walked out of the apartment—and out of our relationship. I was sad to be leaving my husband, yet the feeling of honoring myself was new to me and brought a sense of self-worth and power that I had seldom felt. Rather than giving in to my insecurity and fear of losing Barry, I was honoring the "No" inside me, which gave me the strength to leave him.

I often look back on that time and try to imagine what would have happened if I'd tried to accommodate Barry's desire to experiment with sexual openness with other women. I feel that he would have lost respect for me because I had not been honoring my own inner voice. Had I stayed, it would have been out of fear of losing him, a fear which probably would have driven him further and further away from me. Ironically, by risking the loss of our relationship to honor my own feelings, I ended up finding myself. In the period I was gone, I began to find an inner strength I never knew I had. I began to understand who I really was. I knew I must never ignore my inner being and the guidance that was beginning to flow through me. In many ways, saying "No" in such a strong manner was the conscious beginning of my awakening to my own inner light and God Presence.

SAYING "NO" TO OURSELVES

Perhaps the most important "No" of all is the one that needs to be said to ourselves. This may be even more difficult than saying "No" to our partner because it requires more self-discipline, more looking inside. An inner "No" is necessary to set limits upon our unhealthy desires or our dysfunctional actions. Again, it is just as important an act of self-love and spiritual maturity to say "No" to ourself as it is to say "No" to our partner.

Joyce's walking out on our relationship after my sexual encounter with her friend helped me to learn this lesson better. I was not at the time particularly strong on impulse control, a part of me taking pride in my spontaneity. Yet I needed to learn the difference between spontaneity and impulsiveness. Spontaneity is an expression of real freedom. Impulsiveness merely expresses a lack of control over the desires of the mind or body. Neither was I particularly strong on respecting boundaries, my own or another's, especially when it came to sexual boundaries. I was sincerely wanting to share my love with everyone, but I didn't understand the huge difference between opening my heart to someone and allowing the physical or sexual expression of that loving feeling. I wasn't sensitive to how much pain this was causing Joyce and how much confusion it was causing me.

When Joyce left, I had the chance to see and feel the consequences of having crossed a boundary: *my own soul-shaking pain.* I had no idea that her leaving would cause me so much anguish. I had no idea I was so attached to her and to the relationship. It was this pain that eventually taught me how to respect healthy boundaries. A small child's inquisitiveness leads him to touch a hot stove. The burning pain quickly teaches him not to do it again. In a way, my inquisitiveness caused me to burn myself, and I learned too. I learned how to say "No" to the *inappropriate* expression of my sexual desire, *actions which created suffering or confusion in myself and others.*

One year after our brief separation (it was the longest week of my life), I found myself attracted to another woman. I had the opportunity to look at the whole phenomenon in a more conscious way. I was a psychiatry resident, and Rachel was on staff with me. I saw the attraction that existed between us, an attraction that naturally arose from mutual caring and respect. I enjoyed working with her, enjoyed being with her, and we spoke openly about our relationship. Joyce knew all about Rachel and also liked her very much. No boundaries had yet been crossed.

Relationship is such an exquisite teacher and mirror. I have always tried to be an avid student, eager to learn from every opportunity set in front of me. Well, here was another one. One day, Rachel and I were having lunch together at work and happened to be all alone. Looking into her eyes, I became aware that we were moving into a private place—a place that definitely excluded Joyce. I had just crossed a boundary. Had Joyce been sitting next to us, she would surely have felt uncomfortable and excluded from our connection. Fortunately, because of the lessons learned after my affair and because of my own growth, I was acutely aware of all of this.

At the same time, I had a rare but startlingly real glimpse into a potential future. I was at one of those choice points that can completely change the course of our lives. I could actually see myself becoming deeply involved with Rachel. I could see what it would be like to have her as a partner. I could see past the newness of the romantic sexual honeymoon period. Yes, I could even see some basic personality conflicts that I had ignored up to that point. I could see that this relationship with Rachel would not serve either of us in the highest way. And I could see the pain all three of us would feel. It was an illuminating experience. In that moment, I made the conscious choice to say "No" to romantic involvement with Rachel and thus to say "Yes" to our continuing friendship. It was one of those soul victories that brings such sweet joy.

And what about my attraction to Rachel? Was it diminished by my decision? Did it go away? Not at all. I have learned that attraction is much deeper than the physical or the romantic feelings. It is an inner process of soul recognition, almost as if the two people involved are friends being reunited. The key here is that *attraction to someone other than our partner is not a bad or immoral experience.* The conflict arises when we think we have to act on our feelings. Our cultural upbringing tells us we have to *do* something about our feelings of attraction, but *there is nothing that needs to be done*. We don't ever need to act upon these (or any) feelings. All we need to do is feel what we feel, enjoy what we feel, and learn from what we feel. This was the real freedom of expression that I had always been seeking. And this freedom hinged upon my being able to say "No."

Nowadays, I sometimes travel by myself to lead workshops. Such work brings me into close contact with a large number of men and women. I enjoy these connections, which become ever so much sweeter because, in my heart, I include Joyce in them. When I hug another woman, Joyce is there with me. It's not anything I have to work to do. There is so much depth in my relationship with Joyce that I naturally want to carry her into all that I do. When I feel a strong connection with someone, I often recognize qualities about that person that are somehow familiar. This person may feel like an old friend, a brother or sister, a daughter or son, a father or mother, and yes, even a lover from another time or place. I enjoy that recognition and feel no need to act upon it in a way that would cross boundaries and violate the sacred trust I have with Joyce.

I am continually learning the sometimes subtle difference between sex and love. I am learning to say "No" to my impulsiveness, which often requires giving myself reflective time between thought and action. By doing this, I am learning how to say "Yes" to more real love and spontaneity in my life. I am creating deeper relationships with others, but most of all, without my boundary confusion, I am creating a safe and sacred relationship with Joyce.

There are many other ways of saying "No" to ourselves that will bless our relationships. For example, there are times when my feeling of responsibility in the office, taking care of business, becomes more important than loving myself and my family. This is workaholism. Whenever I can say "No" to office work, setting healthy limits on my time there when it is clear that Joyce or the children need me more, it is a victory for my soul.

For our relationships to work, they need to become a priority in our lives, which means saying "No" to the many distractions that pull on our attention and pull us out of our hearts. A healthy relationship needs a lot of time and energy. The media has not done a good job of teaching us this. Some people spend more time nurturing their new car than their partner. Others spend more time nurturing business contacts or acquaintances than their spouse. When we allow ourselves to give too much of our time to less important matters, our primary relationship will suffer. Saying "No," setting limits when it is clear that these other matters can wait, will bless and nourish our relationship.

SAYING "NO" WITH LOVE

A "No" can be hard to hear and hard to say. Barry and I understand that it is often a challenge to find the right way to say it. There are times when "No" needs to be said with strength and power. There are other times when it needs to be said with gentleness and tenderness. An example is when your partner approaches you wanting sexual intimacy. Of course, there will be times when you will be open to sex, but there will also be times when you are not ready or willing for sexual closeness. What happens then? If you go along with your partner's advances out of fear of making them hurt or angry, it will surely backfire. If you really feel "No" inside, yet go along anyway, both of you will feel distant from one another after the experience.

If you feel little desire for sexual intimacy, but feel a "Yes" inside because you want to give to your partner, the experience can become a positive one. You are then acting on a "Yes," an inner go-ahead, which gives power to your actions.

The problem in so many relationships is how to say "No" when your partner is coming toward you with hugs and kisses or "loving" words, and you feel their sexual desire more than their love. How do you say "No" without rejecting them or hurting their feelings?

The first step is to realize that you have a right to say "No." Many times people feel so badly about themselves because they are saying "No" that their response comes across as rigid or angry. With this kind of response, your partner is more likely to feel rejected and hurt. The feeling behind your words has hurt your lover more than the actual words. Your real challenge is to feel good about yourself when you want or need to say "No." When you learn to love yourself when saying "No," your response will be much more clear. Try putting as much love and tenderness into a "No" response as you would into a "Yes" response.

When Barry approaches me sexually and I am not feeling receptive, I try to acknowledge and appreciate his affection and love. I often give him a big hug and kiss, and then let him know that I am either too tired physically or concerned about something that would keep me from really being with him. We both try to put a lot of love into those "No" times so that neither of us feels rejected or hurt. Sometimes I feel such clarity in my "No" response that I may start giggling at how funny we are. Barry especially appreciates this good-natured humoring of our behavior, so different from the destructive effects of sarcastic comments.

This is a simple process. However, it took us a long time to understand how to say "No" in a positive way. If you don't succeed the first time, and your partner feels hurt by your "No" response, just keep on perfecting your skill. When you both learn to say "No" with love, your relationship will rise to a higher level of trust and understanding.

What about those times when a "No" response from your partner arises from a feeling of fear? It takes great sensitivity and love to handle this type of "No." Sometimes it is best to honor the "No," even though you understand it is coming from a place of fear. Other times you can gently reassure your partner and perhaps he or she will begin to discuss the fear.

As Barry mentioned earlier, when he first suggested that we begin working with groups of people, I immediately said, "No." Public speaking had always terrified me. Barry gently opened a space for me to talk about my fear. He encouraged and supported me to try the experience of working with groups. At the end of our conversation, I still sincerely did not want to, but was willing to try. He believed I could speak in front of others and was willing to walk me through the fear. He did. I still sometimes feel nervous before I speak to a large group but, after I get going, I have a great time expressing my thoughts and feelings.

It takes patience for you to respond to a "No" when you believe it comes from your partner's fear. If your partner closes you off or gets angry at you when you try to help them overcome their fear, then you have probably pushed them too much. You may not have demonstrated enough acceptance and sensitivity.

Listening to our own inner feeling is the greatest gift we can give to ourself, to our partner, or to anyone with whom we are in a relationship. If this inner feeling points in a direction of not doing something, then follow that up with a sincere "No." When a "No" answer comes deeply from the heart, it can be gentle, compassionate, and yet powerful. In the long run, a "No" answer coming from inner truth will serve to bring two people closer together.

Listen inside, and don't be afraid to say "No" if your heart is calling you to. A "No" can thus become the solid foundation from which a "Yes" can reach to the stars.

SAYING "NO"

Is there a "No" you need to say to someone? Are you afraid of hurting their feelings? Of the scene it might cause?

If you feel a "No," then you need to practice saying it. Imagine saying it with clarity and kindness. Remember, you have a right to your feelings, which includes the "No." Now feel the power and the love that flows into you as a result of speaking your truth.

Next, is there a "No" you need to say to yourself? To something you are doing which is interfering with your own or your relationship's highest good? Imagine saying "No" to yourself with the same clarity and kindness that you used

saying it to your friend. Again, feel how you are really saying "Yes" to your own soul, saying "Yes" to having love as a
priority in your life.

Make a commitment to practice this often.

14

Passion and Compassion

*My heart has become an ocean, beloved, since you
have poured your love into it.*

—HAZRAT INAYAT KHAN

S EX CAN BE A PHYSICALLY ECSTATIC, deeply emotional, and spiritually fulfilling experience. How a man and a woman
approach each sexual experience can be quite different, but
with patience and care, both can equally share the richness
of lovemaking.

Sex is and has always been a beautiful part of our relationship, yet it
has not been without work. Barry and I write from many years of learning to bring a higher consciousness and heart connection into our sexual relationship, hoping that this work can reach out to inspire others.

We have a monogamous sexual relationship. We save the sexual
experience to share only with each other. We feel this sexual sharing
with each other is blessed and have learned there is a deep level of
trust that is built through monogamy that makes the sexual experience more deeply fulfilling.

I once heard a man who had been married for a long time compare his monogamous relationship with eating a gourmet meal, which has been lovingly prepared using high quality, life-giving ingredients. This meal is served on a beautifully decorated table. One feels like an honored and special guest while being seated. The meal is both delicious and deeply satisfying. He then compared multiple sexual partners with eating in a fast-food restaurant. "The experience of eating may fill the stomach, may even taste good," he said, "but leaves the soul unsatisfied." In a monogamous relationship, where the sexual act is approached with love and respect, a sacred trust can build, and the "gourmet" experience can become more wonderful year after year.

Knowing absolutely in my mind and heart that I will never seek an outside sexual partner for excitement or fulfillment has allowed the sexual experience with Barry to become profoundly beautiful. Knowing Barry is doing the same causes my heart to open even more in love and in the desire to give.

We also understand that we approach the sexual experience in different ways. Sometimes, with just one kiss, Barry can be ready to hop into bed. I may have similarly enjoyed the kiss, but could just as easily go take a walk together or share in a meaningful conversation. There are many times when we do end up sharing time nonsexually. Sometimes he easily gives up his desire. Sometimes he doesn't, and my suggestion of alternate activities are met with gentle persistence on his part. The question is, do I really not want to make love, or am I just not in the same mood as Barry but would like to be? Knowing each other as we do, he knows this little dialogue that goes on inside me. He knows I won't enter into the sexual experience unless it feels right, but he also knows that sometimes all I need is a little patient caring to help me join his desire.

"How about a little back rub?" he offers, smiling. That is a line he has used so many times it makes us both laugh. Sometimes I accept the back rub even though I know he may have hopes of more. While rubbing my back, he also starts appreciating me. When I say "Yes" to the back rub, I am also saying "Yes" to this genuine flow of love from Barry. He is patient with me and seems content to go on rubbing my back and appreciating me forever. He doesn't pressure me in any way.

It sometimes doesn't take long before my desire is to kiss and let our bodies melt into one another. I need that extra acceptance, of love without pressure, and permission to say "No" at any time. Sometimes the back rub relaxes me so much, I feel like going to sleep. Barry accepts this too.

Occasionally, I am the one to approach Barry sexually. This is so unexpected that he rarely refuses and is often thrilled by the whole idea. There are many times when we are both in the same mood together from the beginning. These are indeed beautiful times of allowing the expression of love to flow through our bodies together.

Communicating and making eye contact through the sexual experience is important to us both. We try to share the experience rather than one of us going off on our own "trip." We often stop and appreciate each other. These verbal exchanges deepen our heart connection.

Our ultimate purpose in joining together sexually is to merge spiritually. Through prayer, eye contact, communication, honoring, and respect, the sexual experience joins our hearts together in ecstatic oneness and brings us into contact with the source of our being. We feel our purpose in being together and a welling up within us of the great love of the universe that allowed us to find each other. Each sexual union is a powerful reminder of the union of our hearts and souls.

THE SECRET GARDEN

Sex has always been an important part of Joyce's and my relationship. On our first date, our eighteen-year-old hands found one another's in a darkened movie theater and sent thrills through our bodies. Later that same evening, as Joyce shared earlier, our lips touched briefly in a good-bye kiss, and we glimpsed in that moment the deepest places our souls could travel. As it is for so many new lovers, the flow of our sexual energy opened the doors to a higher dimension, allowing us to breathe the fragrant aromas of a secret inner garden. Sex was a powerful and spiritual experience.

Still a teenage boy, I became initiated into the sweetness of this overwhelming energy of creation. So powerful was this sexually induced awakening that I quickly became addicted to the heavenly nectar. From the beginning of my relationship with Joyce, I could not keep my hands off her—something that has not changed much in thirty years, although now I tend to be more sensitive to right timing, and to Joyce's needs as well as my own.

I smile when I think of our son, John-Nuriel. When he was nursing, Joyce's breasts were his "neenee." When he was three years old, he was obsessed with having his hands on his mama's breasts. At that point dry and of course softer, the breasts became his "gushies." His admiration was innocent. He just wanted to be in that heavenly state in which nursing allowed him to dwell. Joyce's breasts were the physical connection to that memory.

In a way, the sexual experience, the closeness of my body to Joyce's, and the deep sensual feelings have always been a way I nursed on the breasts of a wondrous mother, a divine creative being. I remember how hard it was to be separated from Joyce for our last two years of college. Every few weeks, we would visit for a weekend and spend almost the whole time "nursing." In these early years of our relationship, our physical connection was an all-important means for tapping into a spiritual dimension of being, for feeling the powerful energies of love.

We now know the deepest desire permeating our sexual relationship has always been to feel love. Over the years, we have learned nonsexual ways to connect with the source of that love, our spiritual essence, such as meditation, prayer, sharing our feelings and thoughts, or serving others in our work. In this way, our lives are becoming more balanced, with less urgency for fulfillment placed on sex. Our physical connection, however, is still as important and magical as ever because of this balance.

Our sexual relationship, just like our relationship in general, has not been without problems. At times, as I mentioned above, I placed too much importance on physical intimacy as *the* way to fulfillment, and my expectations would sabotage the experience. Rather than lovemaking being a natural expression of our closeness, I was trying to use sex as *the* way to feel closer to Joyce—and to my own heart. I was trying to use another person (Joyce) to give me the experience of loving myself, instead of turning within for this self-love. This approach can never work. Devoid of love, no physical or outward method can gain access to spiritual or inner realms. To try to do so is to use sex as an addictive substance, which is *abuse*—not use. Love, in the form of caring, respect, sensitivity, and deep listening, must be present for the sexual experience to be a magical experience. In other words, *sex by itself does not create love. It is love which creates more love.*

Other times, Joyce and I became confused about the various spiritual teachings about sexuality. We once tried celibacy as the highest spiritual path. We felt it was a spiritual accomplishment when we once lasted six months without sex. And we didn't even know why we were getting such severe headaches!

At the time, we viewed our natural sexual desire as a downward force which was depleting us of our vital energy. This was confirmed by those times when our sexual experiences were less spiritual and more physical, with more animal-like passion, and we would feel drained afterward. We didn't understand that it was the lack of love in the sex that drained us—not the sex itself. For when love was present before, during, and after the physical act, our energy was increased, not depleted.

When we finally realized that celibacy was not our highest sexual *or* spiritual option, our bodies came together in an explosion of passion. This presented our next dilemma: allowing the earthy, physical energy to coexist with the love—feeling our passion *and* our compassion. Sometimes the passion would be so overwhelming that we would get lost in the physical sensations. The orgasm, then, would be more of a physical release than a merging into union. Even though these times were less conscious of loving, we needed to learn not to judge ourselves or "grade" each sexual experience. There is nothing inherently wrong with passionate, physical sex. It is our judging mind that creates the biggest problems. We are human as well as spiritual beings. Our growth depends upon our acceptance of ourselves where we are, rather than where we would like to be. In our souls, we hold a memory of the highest love and sensual ecstasy. Our work is to be more gentle with ourselves when our experience on Earth doesn't quite reflect that same remembered perfection.

Joyce and I are continually learning about passion and compassion. We are becoming more sensitive to our intention before lovemaking. We are learning how to set our inner sights on deepening our love, allowing every part of the experience to be a part of that deepening. We are learning how to enjoy the journey thoroughly and not place our emphasis upon arriving at a particular goal. We are learning how to pray with thankful hearts before, during, and after lovemaking. We are learning how to move slowly, to savor each morsel of the meal, even to stop all movement to integrate all that has happened up to that point. We are learning how to feel the full intensity of delicious passion in our hearts well up with the fullness of compassionate love. We are learning how to tune into one another's experience, to enjoy what the other is enjoying, and therefore to wait joyfully for the other to enter the ripeness just before orgasm. And we are learning how to allow orgasm to be an implosion rather than an explosion, feeling the light of creation fill every cell of our bodies as our two hearts become one.

How Soon Do You Make Love?

A man in his thirties once shared that he was in a new relationship and, naturally, the thought of sex came up frequently. He admitted that, in the past, he had pressed for sexual involvement early in the relationship but felt acting on his urgency had not been beneficial. He wanted to know when it was right to enter into a sexual relationship.

First, we need to realize there is no start or finish to the sexual relationship. In *The Shared Heart*, we included a chapter on the sexual relationship called "Making Love to God." This may be a startling title to some people, but if we want our relationships to be all that they can be, we need to start thinking of sex in much bigger terms.

Sexuality involves a flow of love, of life-force, through our being. We get hung up about sex because we equate it with only the physical expression of lovemaking. But sex is so much more than a physical act. The moment we look deeply into another's eyes, the times we are vulnerable, letting ourselves be clearly seen in our weakness and our strength, these are all sexual as well as spiritual moments. This is all lovemaking.

So, you may ask, if a relationship is always sexual as well as spiritual, then why wait at all before entering into the physical act of lovemaking?

When our son, John-Nuriel, was a newborn infant, Joyce and I were intrigued by watching this tiny being grow and change. We were awed by the timing of the universe. Just like with our two older children, we reverently watched John-Nuri's gradual transition into the physical world. In the beginning, there was a heavenly sweetness as his awareness drifted freely in and out of his newborn body. Then gradually, he became grounded, more and more present in the physical world, more and more alert and aware of his body.

It is much the same with a new relationship. There is often the same heavenly sweetness as two souls begin to share love. There is inspiration and ecstasy from this nonphysical joining. Then gradually, as a natural evolution, the relationship comes down to Earth. It moves from the higher, spiritual realms to include the psychological and emotional and then, finally, the physical dimension. To hurry this process is as unnatural as hurrying a baby into its body. In a sense, a baby's soul has the same courtship with its body that two souls have as they cultivate their friendship. This courting process is important to the relationship. It develops the level of trust needed as the relationship dives into the physical expression, where it is easier to lose sight of the inspiration and purpose of the relationship. Without this trust, this cultivated friendship, it is like taking a new boat directly out to sea without first trying it out in the calmer waters of the harbor.

We have consistently seen new relationships get into trouble because the two individuals involved have not been sensitive to this natural evolution of sexuality. Sometimes the sensitivity required can be subtle. The couple may *think* they're ready for lovemaking. To them, their relationship seems fully mature and ripe. New love has a way of putting filters in front of our eyes, of making it seem like we're much further along than we really are. Yet these feelings of readiness are often based more on illusion and physical desire than the highest truth for each of us and for our relationship.

Premature lovemaking is a little like taking a psychedelic drug. It may give us an approximation of love, but it can only be an approximation. It is not the real thing. Real love is an experience that must be earned through life experiences and the maturity of our souls. But this is so typical of human nature; we're so often in a hurry for love. We try to force love. Jesus' parable of the wedding feast is a great example. In this parable, a man tries to enter a wedding feast without the proper attire. He is not ready for the feast, has not prepared himself for it. He is, of course, thrown out, and there is "much gnashing of teeth" (suffering) as a result. There are natural consequences to our forcing open the sensitive door of sexuality without proper preparation. This often results in loss of trust, loss of safety, and loss of love.

How will you know if you have waited long enough to make love? You'll feel a deep trust with one another. Will you ruin this trust if you have sex and it turns out to be too soon? Of course not. All of relationship is a process of trying to listen within, acting on what you think you hear or feel, making lots of mistakes, and then humbly trying again. If you make love too soon and feel it has taken something away from your closeness or frightened some part of you, talk about it. Open, honest communication of your feelings is the way to regain trust and renew friendship. You may both decide to wait a little longer before you make love again. There is nothing wrong with waiting. It doesn't mean you or your relationship are a failure. Trial and error is a valid method of learning and gaining experience.

Our continual encouragement to couples who want to live in the highest state of love is this: Spend as much time as you both need to cultivate friendship and trust before entering into the physical expression of sexuality. The act of lovemaking will come and go, but the friendship is eternal.

Bringing Back the Passion

Many people in long-term relationships have shared that they miss the intensity and passion their lovemaking had when they were first together. They ask us how they can bring these qualities back.

First of all, we need to let go of the Hollywood image of the sexual relationship. According to this image, there is no room for lovemaking to grow and change—the Hollywood ideal is a static ideal. Whether we are in a brand-new relationship or celebrating our golden anniversary, sex is somehow supposed to be the same.

But how can this be, if other aspects of our relationships are constantly changing? As a relationship evolves, so does sexuality. So the challenge is not a matter of regaining something that was lost. It's more a matter of finding the next level of sexual expression, an expression which is in tune with who we are now.

What about the nature of sexual attraction? Sometimes sexual attraction arises out of the desire for distraction and excitement. We all sometimes have this desire, to be entertained, stimulated, aroused—*by our partner.* Taking it deeper, we all sometimes want another person to take care of us, rather than taking responsibility for ourselves. But ultimately, if we want to grow spiritually, *all that we want another to do for us we must do for ourselves.*

Here again is the mirror at work. When we feel sexual attraction *for another person*, it really means that we have allowed that person to catalyze an opening or a flow of energy through our body. It is really *we* who opened to this divine, creative energy of life. So on the deepest level, it is *we* who turn ourselves on and *we* who need to accept responsibility for this beautiful flow of love-energy in our own body and consciousness. By saying this, we are not referring to self-pleasuring, although there may be a need for this at certain times in an individual's life. We are speaking about taking responsibility for where love originates. *It comes from within our hearts, not from another person.* Therefore, to bring sexual passion back into our relationship, we need to recognize that it comes from within us, not from our partner.

Some people may assume that, as their relationship ages, they need to let go of intensity and passion. This is not true. We are meeting an increasing number of senior citizens—not to mention couples in their middle years—whose sexual relationships are anything but dull and lifeless. So what is their secret? They have found that intensity and passion are a way of life, a state of consciousness, rather than just an expression of sexuality. They live life intensely and passionately. They appreciate one another passionately. They are committed to sharing their feelings with one another. They make time for their relationship. They don't let minor irritations or resentments slip by without working them through. They have focused on making every part of their relationship intense and passionate, and so this same attitude is carried over to their lovemaking.

The sexual expression in a relationship continues to grow and evolve. As the relationship matures, the lovemaking can more and more take on a spiritual dimension. It can become more open, more conscious, more love-filled. It can become more integrated with the rest of the relationship. Although there is more gratification for the soul, this does not mean that it is less sensual or pleasurable. On the contrary, the sensuality can become more intense—but it is a deeper and more mature sensuality. Bringing our soul, bringing every part of us, into our lovemaking allows for the highest levels of sensuality.

We often mistakenly think of sensuality as pertaining to the body, but what about emotional sensuality? There is intense pleasure with the deep sharing of feelings and thoughts. What about spiritual ecstasy—the ultimate sensual experience? The experience of radiant energy, the light of God, flowing through our body is intensely pleasurable. Joyce and I have had times, especially after a meditation, of ecstatic union while simply gazing into one another's eyes. In such moments, the feeling of love in our hearts is accompanied by deep sensual pleasure in our bodies, all without the slightest physical contact. And we are not alone in having these experiences. It gives us great joy to hear from more and more couples who are reaching these spiritual levels of sensuality and sexuality. Such ecstasy is available to everyone.

PLEASE JUST HOLD ME!

Marty and Sheila were stuck. And they were stuck like many couples Joyce and I have seen in our counseling sessions and workshops. Sex just wasn't working. Marty was feeling sexually frustrated, continually disappointed in Sheila's lack of interest in sex.

I asked Sheila what she was needing. She thought for a moment, then replied, "I just need to be held by Marty." It was hard for Sheila to say that, just like it is hard for many people to give voice to their deeper needs. Both men and women often feel guilty about their need for nonsexual touch, as if there were something wrong with them for not being instantly sexually available to their partner. We discovered that for Sheila, as for many women, there is a deep need to experience the love of a father, the safe, non-pressuring nurturing and acceptance from a man. It's not that Sheila was against having sex with Marty; she in fact expressed strong feelings of attraction for him. Their relationship had simply progressed to the point where Sheila's deeper needs were coming to the surface, and she could no longer suppress them.

What about Marty's frustration? For Marty, as with many (but definitely not all) men, the sexual act was perhaps the main way he gave and received nurturing in the relationship. He needed to learn how to give and receive love in other, nonsexual ways. He needed to practice active and compassionate listening, sharing his inner self and more vulnerable feelings, and nonsexual touch and holding. A key for Marty, as it is for many men, was becoming aware of his own need for the nurturing of a mother. It is natural for little boys to transition from total dependence upon their mothers to a pushing-away stage of growth in a move toward self-reliance. But eventually, all boys need to come to terms with their need for the nurturing love of the mother. It is really the nurturing love of the mother-father, or parent archetype, that we seek. It is somewhat artificial to separate parental nurturing into one or another sex.

So as Marty opened to his need for this parental nurturing love, which can come through Sheila, he became more vulnerable to her.

As he allowed himself to be held and nurtured as a child, he became able to hold and nurture Sheila's inner child, which she needed. In other words, as he accepted the deeper needs of his own inner child, he is able to accept similar needs in another.

Sheila needed to give a clear and guilt-free voice to her inner child. She needed to know it is OK to need nonsexual nurturing. As she understood the acceptability of her soul's needs, she was able to communicate them more clearly—without anger, withdrawal, depression, or however else these unaccepted feelings come to the surface. Furthermore, as she accepted the needs of her own inner child, she could in turn accept the needs of Marty's inner child. This put her more in touch with her nurturing self, her own parent archetype.

When there is enough nonsexual expression of caring in a relationship, then the sexual expression can be more fulfilling. When the soul, as well as the inner child, feels safe and nurtured, and when the heart is open to love, then the body can become ready to feel the highest levels of ecstasy.

I had Marty and Sheila practice the following exercise. For them, it was a major revelation and helped them deeply. May it also help you.

NONSEXUAL HOLDING

Create a special time for nonsexual holding. Make it clear that this time will absolutely *not* lead to physical sex. This is especially important when there has been broken trust or other difficulty in the sexual relationship. It is critical when there has been a history of childhood sexual trauma.

Take turns holding one another as a loving parent would hold a small child who needs to be held. Share your feelings with one another—both as the child needing to be held and as the parent needing to hold a child.

Let this be a safe time of pure nurturing and being nurtured.

15

The Dance of Jealousy

*The glory of friendship is not the outstretched hand,
nor the kindly smile, nor the joy of companionship;
it is the spiritual inspiration that comes to one when
he discovers that someone else believes in him and is
willing to trust him.*

—RALPH WALDO EMERSON

JEALOUSY IS A CHALLENGE THAT MOST PEOPLE WILL FACE at one time or another. When both partners work together to overcome this challenge, they can grow closer in love and understanding. When jealously is labeled as one person's fault, however, a problem is created that can be difficult to overcome. To blame jealousy on our partner is to refuse to see them as a soul mirror, reflecting our part of this dance. It is important to understand that most problems with jealousy are a co-creation of both partners in the relationship, and are usually symptoms of deeper dysfunction in the relationship—an outer reflection of two soul's insecurities.

As we have explained earlier, when Barry ended his psychiatry residency in 1973, we traveled for over a year studying from various spiritual teachers. Our pilgrimage took us to the French Alps to learn from Pir Vilayat Khan, a Sufi teacher. We lived in a camp in an Alpine meadow high in the mountains for two months. This was the first time in our nine-year relationship that we lived so closely with so many people (over 200), most of whom were single. At the time, I was still quite shy and preferred to be with Barry and perhaps one or two other people. Barry, on the other hand, was just experiencing his newly regained wings of freedom. Medical school and residency had been intensely confining for him. He was now sensing an inner exuberance that had yet to be fully unleashed.

Our teacher, Pir Vilayat, sensed my quiet inner nature and suggested I spend as much time as possible alone in meditation. This I gladly did and received much benefit. He had also sensed Barry's need to be with others and asked him to be the camp doctor. Barry accepted, and set about his task with great enthusiasm. There were many medical problems, and he made deep connections with many people. Unfortunately, it seemed to me most of these connections were with attractive, available women. Feelings of jealousy began to grow in me that I had never felt before.

Once, during a meal, Barry got up from our table to talk to an attractive woman about her medical problem. It seemed to me like a long enough time had elapsed, so I got up from the table and stood by Barry. I felt he ignored my presence on purpose. He later said he didn't know I was there. It was true that I didn't say anything. Meanwhile, the woman was shooting looks of annoyance my way. It seemed obvious to me that this woman saw me as a threat to her newly established relationship with Barry. I also realized she had no idea I was Barry's wife. Jealousy tore through my heart. I wasn't afraid that Barry would be sexual with this woman. We had already worked that out in our relationship. I felt excluded, somehow, stranded on the outside of the circle of their relating.

Finally I blurted out, "I'm Barry's wife," my voice betraying the jealousy I was feeling. The woman looked shocked and quickly stammered, "I didn't know Barry was married." Then she walked away.

I glared at Barry, my jealousy giving way to anger. Barry didn't know what he had done wrong and was upset with me for acting so immaturely. He didn't understand why I was feeling jealous and angry. I did. I was angry at him for being so friendly to everyone, but I was really angry at myself. I thought I had the bigger problem.

After that, Barry became more friendly and outgoing; I became more withdrawn and quiet. We both assumed I had a problem with jealousy and that Barry was innocent in his interactions with the women. Barry seemed happy on the outside, and forged ahead making new friends, but I could see that the growing distance between us saddened him also. It was impossible for me to really love him as long as we both thought I was "the problem."

We began going off by ourselves between classes trying to seek a resolution. As long as the focus was on me and *my problem*, the distance remained. Then one day, I stopped and asked myself this question: "What is really hurting me in this situation with Barry?" I realized what hurt me most was not that Barry had all these new women friends, but that I felt excluded and unacknowledged as his wife. Barry's role in the "jealousy problem" emerged—*he was not including me in his new friendships*. He would neglect to tell these women that he was married, while at the same time choosing not to wear his wedding ring. From the beginning of our marriage, he had insisted the ring was uncomfortable on his finger. Nevertheless, the ring's absence seemed to hint at a deeper discomfort in Barry, adding to my insecurity in the marriage.

When we now look back to that time, we can see what was happening on a deeper level. I still felt insecure about Barry's devotion and commitment to me and my worthiness to be loved by him. I was not, however, the only insecure one. Barry still felt insecure about his need for my love, so he perceived a kind of safety in reaching out to other women. It had only been a year or two since we had consciously set out on a journey toward spiritual growth, after the major crisis of the affair. We were pretty new at this "growth" business.

At the time, even with our limited awareness of what was happening, we agreed that whenever I approached Barry while he was with one of his new friends, he would greet me warmly and introduce me. Barry also decided to tell each new friend right away about our relationship. I decided I would hold in my heart the feeling of how much Barry really did love me, and remember to feel worthy of being included in his new friendships.

The next time I happened upon him giving medical advice to a woman, I walked right up and put my arms around him. Barry hugged me back and introduced me. A warm feeling flowed between me and the woman. I realized she was going to become *my* friend as well.

Our new pattern added an unexpected and important dimension to Barry's life, as well. Through his acknowledgment of our relationship and love, his friendships with women deepened. Women felt safer to be friends with him; they knew where they stood with him. In addition, my new confidence in myself and the relationship allowed me to more appreciate Barry's outgoing, friendly manner. Soon I was out meeting new friends and introducing them to Barry.

Since that time, whenever jealousy has become an issue, we have returned to the lessons we learned during our stay in the Alps: *Jealousy is never one person's problem. Both contribute to the dance.* When two people are growing in love and commitment, each partner needs to know they are safe in the other's presence. Each individual needs to know they will not be excluded no matter where their partner goes. And if they do feel excluded, they need to know they can work together to resolve the feelings and the situation. Most of all, each partner needs to feel acknowledged and loved—and validated for whatever feelings they have.

It is important to continually look for ways to include your beloved in your life. Once, at a party, I became deeply engrossed in conversation with a male friend. We must have been talking for more than half an hour when Barry came and sat down with us. He had been in the backyard playing with all the children, and was in a silly, giggly mood. Our friend had just started sharing some painful issues in his life. Our serious and heartfelt conversation contrasted sharply with Barry's lightness. I welcomed Barry and explained the situation. He knew he had a choice to join us in our conversation or go and laugh some more with the children. Barry chose to stay and soon had moved into our state of feeling, adding valuable insight. Had our friend and I excluded Barry, jealousy and tension might have occurred. Instead, we offered a way in for him—as well as the choice of coming.

The fear and hurt of being excluded is perhaps one of the main reasons why nonmonogamous relationships are rarely successful. Can you imagine quite innocently entering a room where your partner is having sex with someone else? Is your beloved going to smile at you and let you know you are welcome? Probably not! The unwelcome feeling in such a situation hurts deeply, and is difficult to move beyond. The sexual act is so deeply intimate between two people that it is almost impossible to overcome feelings of jealousy at being left out.

Trying to hold your heart open to your partner at all times is a wonderful practice. I know I am safe to enter whatever connection Barry has with another person. I feel I'll be received with respect. Barry, likewise, feels the same. The door of our hearts is always open to one another, creating a sence of safety that allows our hearts to merge ever more deeply in love.

16

Gifts from Disappointment

Learn that eternity is now. There is no past or present or future as separate periods of time. All is within the soul's embrace now. It is the reaction to the now which is your future. Never look into the future and anticipate this, that or the other, for to do so is to live in fear. Live today with God, and your future can hold nothing but joy.

—White Eagle

HOW MANY TIMES HAS IT HAPPENED THAT you have planned a special time with your beloved, and it hasn't worked out the way you wanted? Perhaps you expected and hoped an activity would go a certain way, and it didn't. Maybe you were prepared for a loving, romantic evening, and your lover fell asleep. Perhaps you planned a wonderful picnic, and your husband forgot. Maybe you needed a time of deep communion, and your wife showed up consumed with worries and unable to relax. Perhaps you were hoping to bring a magical touch into your relationship, and your mate didn't even notice. Such events occur all the time in relationships.

How do we work with disappointment? When we are seeking a special time, one that has elements of wonder, deep communion, and magic, we tend to believe we are seeking connection with someone else. But this is not the case. We are really seeking a connection with our spirit. It is our soul's desire to be in deeper connection with our heavenly condition. The inner cry of every soul, no matter how faint, is to reexperience the wonder, ecstasy, joy, and magical quality of our source. When we desire and plan for this level of connection with our partner, we are really responding to an inner call to feel our true essence.

There are times when our partner is right there with us, desiring that depth of connection and wanting to feel the wonder of our love together. These can be beautiful times in which there is no limit to the pure love that we can both feel. However, it doesn't always work out that way. Sometimes our partner is just not in the same mood we are or is not feeling in that moment the same desire or need for depth. Perhaps this scenario reverses itself another time, with our partner feeling the need when we are not.

These disappointments in relationship are a day-to-day challenge, especially for the one who is desiring, planning, and expecting a special time. What do you do when you have planned a special evening? Romantic music is playing. You have put on clothes your partner has appreciated in the past. The children are sent off with friends. Your partner comes home, doesn't notice you, and turns on the TV. Perhaps you then turn off the TV, in an effort to get his attention. In your most loving voice, you explain how the children are gone and you would like to have a special evening with him. Your partner looks tired and weary from the day and points to a place on the couch, inviting you to share in the couch-potato experience. You explain, that isn't what you want. Your partner gets up to turn on the TV, telling you (in as kind a voice as possible) that he is tired and just wants to be left alone.

Now what do you do? You could watch TV, which you know will

not satisfy your soul's need for connection. You could get angry at your partner, running him down with all the energy you have put into planning and expecting a special evening. This will probably make the evening miserable for both of you.

Or you could realize that your desire for connection and a sense of magic is really for your own life. You need to understand the intention behind your plan. You need to feel connected with your *own* soul and spiritual essence. You need to feel your own magic and sense of wonder, rather than projecting your need for fulfillment onto your partner. Your partner has to listen to his or her own call for depth and connection. You could sulk because your partner won't join in, or you could take this opportunity to truly love yourself and honor your own spiritual essence by having a special evening all by yourself.

Our souls have such a need for this time alone for inner connection. This innate desire often manifests itself through wanting to share that spiritual feeling with our partner. This is beautiful and necessary in relationship, but is not always possible. People go through different states of consciousness all the time. It is disappointing when your partner doesn't have the same desire in a given moment for closeness. This disappointment can devastate us, or it can awaken us to our own need for spiritual union with our inner being.

These times of disappointment can be a real opportunity for inner growth. As your inner communion deepens, and you are loving your true essence more fully, you will also be given the understanding of how to awaken your partner's desire for connection. This will come about through love, not force. As you learn how to romance yourself, your partner will be drawn to you in a natural and magnetic way.

I have had similar experiences with Barry, only it wasn't the TV that got in the way. It was work in our home office. When I would finally see that the magical time just wasn't going to happen with him, I would leave the room and sit down in a peaceful place. Then I would have what I call one of my little "talks" with myself. The mother part of me talks to the little girl part of me:

"Joyce, how are you feeling?"

Sometimes tears flow from my little girl self. She feels

disappointed, hurt, or lonely. So I allow my inner mother to hold and comfort my inner little girl. (Try to visualize or feel this for yourself.)

After my inner child's feelings have been expressed, my inner mother asks, "Now what shall we do that would be fun and also help you to connect with the beauty of your soul?"

My little inner girl might still feel upset and rebellious. She might make an unhealthy suggestion, like plotting a way to get even with Barry. My inner mother gently guides my hurt inner child to a more constructive activity.

"How about taking a gratitude walk?" she offers.

This is one of my favorite activities—just walking and thanking God, the ever-present light, for all the blessings in my life. I also enjoy reading some of my favorite inspirational books, like *The Quiet Mind* by White Eagle, and then reflecting on how the words apply to my own life. I enjoy soaking in our hot tub and feeling the beauty of everyone I know, ending with myself. These activities nurture my soul and satisfy my thirst for inner connection.

After being alone in this way for a while, I often feel so happy inside I could dance. I usually return to Barry, who by then may be finished with his work and quite happy to be with me. Without the pressure on him to provide the depth of connection I was needing, he often senses a deeper joy in me and feels attracted to me.

Expectations placed upon ourselves or our partner inevitably lead to disappointment. Having expectations prevents us from allowing people or things to be as they are, and keeps us from living in the present moment. This is very different from a feeling of *expectancy*, which is really a willingness to receive all the good that can possibly come to us. Nevertheless, as long as we are human we will continue to have expectations—and disappointment. Let these expectations serve as a call to awaken us to the need to love ourselves more.

Barry can be an incredibly wise person. He can say things to people that give them inspiration in even the most difficult situations. There was a time in our early years together when I grew to depend on Barry's wisdom. At difficult times, I found myself urgently waiting to talk with him. Sometimes, however, he just wasn't able to be there for me in the way I needed. He might come home tired or upset. Then I would feel disappointed because I felt I needed him to support me.

Over the years, as I waited for Barry to come home each day, I realized that I was actually needing to heed my own inner wisdom. I started shifting my dependence from relying on Barry's wisdom onto my own ability to handle difficult situations. The disappointment that came from knowing Barry could not always be my wise, comforting counselor gave birth to the equally wise counselor within my own heart. Now, I seek that inner place of wisdom first. The wisdom that flows through Barry is like a sweet dessert. The wisdom that flows through my own heart is the sustaining food that gives guidance and fulfillment to all I do.

Relationship gives us the opportunity to grow—if we are willing to see our partner as a mirror reflecting back to us the ways we need to strengthen ourselves from within. If Barry had always been there for me in wisdom and comfort, I would not have learned these valuable lessons of the soul. If our partner were always there to dance with us, we would never learn how to dance alone.

17

Will the Challenges Ever End?

What is to give light must endure burning.

—VIKTOR FRANKL

"I S THERE EVER AN END TO THE PAIN OF LIFE?"

"Will we ever get to the point where there are no issues left to deal with?"

"Will our relationships ever cease to be such hard work?"

"Will this struggle ever stop?"

"Can I just have happiness?"

The answer to all of these frequently asked questions is yes *and* no. Until we feel grateful for the lessons of soul growth that relationship brings, we will continue to experience them as struggle and pain. As we realize that our relationships can be vehicles for taking us into the light, however, the issues cease to be merely painful and become avenues for growth and healing. Until we have this realization and can feel gratitude, the issues and struggles will seem heavier than they really are. When we resist learning our lessons, we miss out on opportunities to grow, heal, and become more beautiful and light-filled.

About fourteen years ago, Barry and I were having a difficult time in our relationship. I remember the pain and feeling of hopelessness that was setting in. It seemed that nothing we did could help us come back into harmony. I was meditating and praying for guidance. Part of me felt we were at the end of our relationship and should just give up.

Day after day, I sat before a small candle and prayed. Finally, the answer came to me clearly: *This is your service to the world.*

The message was short. Too short, I thought. It took me several more days to understand. Our struggle, and our persistence to get through it, was our service to the world in that moment.

We kept on trying and eventually a deep healing took place. We began to feel more love and devotion to each other, and a renewed strength and commitment for our union. We knew we had stepped through one of the great initiations of relationship. Our love had been thoroughly tested and we had persevered. Our relationship had been initiated into greater light.

Shortly after this time, I was sitting alone in the woods while our family was camping. Suddenly, I knew I was not alone. A presence and energy came to me so strongly I felt I could have reached out and touched it. In my heart I heard the words, *You are both ready now. I would like to be born.* Our second daughter was asking to come to Earth.

Around this time, we also received the vision and guidance for our first book. Now I understood the purpose of Barry's and my earlier struggles. The testing period that preceded these two valuable gifts, a new baby and a new book, though difficult and painful, had brought us to a newer and higher level of our relationship. The birth of our second child and the publication of our first book both helped to bring our service to the world. This work with others could not have been as deep and fulfilling without the period of tests and struggle—and our victory.

After our first daughter, Rami, was born, we went through quite an adjustment becoming parents. We had been together for eleven years without children. In addition to being somewhat fixed in our ways, a selfishness had set in that was difficult to overcome. By the time Mira, our second child, was born, we had fairly well made the adjustment into parenting. We both found tremendous joy in raising the girls. We had a number of years of relative calm in our family life.

Then we had a third baby who died before being born. This brought up a whole new set of issues and challenges. Some we met with peaceful gratitude. Some we struggled over. Eventually there was peace and we moved on.

Several years later, we had our first son. Well initiated into parenting, we thought this would be a breeze, but raising a son is different than raising a daughter. Though we love and adore him, John-Nuriel challenges us both in many new ways.

Parenting is definitely one of our current challenges. Just when we think we have John-Nuriel or the girls all handled, up pops another issue. Our children are growing and changing, and we need to change along with them. And we are. Our relationship is growing and changing, and we are grateful for this growth.

We have now been together for over thirty years. There are still issues that bring pain to our relationship. When we remember to be grateful for these challenges and grateful for the growth that they bring, we move through them more quickly. When we resent the disruption to our usually peaceful lives, or blame each other, we have more pain and struggle.

The nature of life, as well as the spiritual path, is change. With change comes challenge and opportunity for healing and growth. We can never expect continual happiness in our relationship or in our lives. When it comes, treat it as a dear, beloved friend, but when a challenge or issue between you seems to cloud your happiness, learn how to be grateful. Remember that within every problem is a gift, an opportunity for deeper growth and healing. By working through the issue, you will know even more joy and happiness. Joy, love, and happiness flow in balance with the challenges. Bring joy into each challenge, and neither the happiness nor the growth seem far away.

Will the challenges stop coming? Probably not. Will the pain ever cease? Probably not. One constant about life and relationship is the ever-new opportunity for deeper love and harmony. When two hearts are filled with gratitude and appreciation, there is no limit to the amount of love and fulfillment that a relationship can bring. This is the key to a lasting love.

HIDDEN BLESSINGS

Either alone or with your partner, think about a significant challenge, obstacle, or something you have overcome in your life or relationship. Remember how difficult, painful, or even hopeless it seemed at the time. Can you now feel the gifts or blessings you have received as a direct result of that challenge or the process of working it through? How has your life or relationship been strengthened? Did the problem give you an opportunity to ask for (and receive) help? Any other gifts?

If you are doing this with your partner, help each other to remember and feel the gifts behind this challenge.

Now, do the same with a current challenge facing you. See if you can discover hidden blessings behind this challenge, gifts which may be coming to you as you embrace the problem as an opportunity rather then resist it as a bother or nuisance.

18

Conscious Sacrifices

Love is a fruit in season at all times, and within reach of every hand. Anyone may gather it and no limit is set. Everyone can reach this love through meditation, spirit of prayer and sacrifice, by an intense inner life.

—MOTHER TERESA

THEME THAT OCCURS AGAIN AND AGAIN IN SACRED literature throughout the world is the concept of conscious sacrifice of personal desire. These sacrifices, letting go of personal desires in the spirit of love and giving, can deepen both a relationship and each individual's capacity to open his or her heart. On the other hand, if the sacrifices are made with resentment or even with a stoic sense of duty, they can damage the relationship and eventually destroy it. There is, then, a major difference between joyful or conscious sacrifice and the sacrifice that denies self in an unhealthy (and perhaps unconscious) way.

Some people leap into unhealthy sacrifices in order to feel loved. They deny their own needs in an effort to please their partner. This type of sacrifice is damaging to the relationship and to each individual. Martha, a woman in one of our workshops, had to work full-time to help pay her husband's education loan. He assured her that as soon as the loan was paid off she could stop working. The promise was very important to her; they had two young children who wanted their mom to be home. After several years, the loan was almost paid off when Martha became pregnant again. She wanted to stay home with the new baby. Her husband subsequently went out and bought a very expensive pleasure boat. The high monthly payments required that Martha continue working, and he sacrificed her desire to stay home with the new baby and two children for his own desire for a new speedboat. Her sacrifice denied her own need and the needs of her children. Martha needed to develop the ability to say "No" and take better care of herself.

On the other hand, there are people who are overly interested in taking care of themselves. The man who bought the boat was more interested in taking care of his own desire for pleasure than in considering his wife and children. In our counseling and workshop experience, we have often heard comments reflecting a selfish attitude:

"I love being with my wife. I just don't want to have her children around."

"I would never leave my friends just because my husband has been offered a great job in another city."

"I would never leave my beautiful home in the country and live in the city just because my fiancée's children are in school there and need their mother. She'll have to live where I live."

The variations on this theme go on and on. When people cling to personal desire, it directly hinders a growing intimacy. When two people are each willing to make sacrifices for the other, their love can grow and deepen.

In 1972, Barry and I lived in Los Angeles. Barry was completing his fourth year of medical school, and I had supported both of us during those four years. For three years, I worked as a nurse in rather unfulfilling jobs. For the most part, I did this willingly and cheerfully as our only source of income. I also went back to school and received a master's degree.

During Barry's fourth year of medical school, I was able to land a dream job—head nurse in charge of a brand-new residential treatment program for boys. The facility lay on a beautiful 3,000 acre ranch donated by Cecil B. DeMille, the famous movie maker. Since part of my responsibility involved hiring the staff, I naturally hired many of my friends. The staff of thirty became like a warm and loving family not only to the boys, but to me as well. I had never before known such joy in a job, never realized it was possible to laugh and play at work. Since Barry was often busy working at the hospital, I spent longer and longer hours at work. I found I was happier there than I was alone at home.

I'll never forget the evening I came home from a truly joyful day at work. Barry greeted me with a big smile and said, "I've been accepted for my residency in psychiatry at the University of Oregon Medical Center in Portland. We'll need to move in two months."

My heart sank. For the first time in my life I was truly happy in my work. I felt needed, important, and loved. I knew this residency offer was important to Barry, but I was tired of following him around the country, tired of making all the sacrifices for his education. I couldn't bear to leave my job.

I blurted out, "I'm not going with you!"

After the initial shock, a respectful and loving silence surrounded us as we both pondered my decision. We talked of frequent visits back and forth, and of Barry returning to Los Angeles after the three-year residency.

Two weeks later, I returned home from work to find Barry waiting for me. He seemed peaceful and resolved when he spoke, "I decided to give up my residency program. It's more important to be with you and continue our relationship in an intimate and close way. You are more important than my career."

I was in awe at the sacrifice Barry had just offered our relationship. He and I both knew that without a residency his medical education was practically worthless. He was not only willing to give up advancing his education, he was essentially willing to give up four years of medical school. I could tell this sacrifice had come from a place deep inside of him. He was at peace and I felt profound respect for him.

One week later, my own decision came from a similar inner place. I gave notice at my job and prepared to move 1,500 miles away to Portland, Oregon. We both had been willing to sacrifice personal desires, and our love was strengthened because of it.

I often reflect on that time in our marriage. Without willingness on both of our parts to sacrifice what was important to us personally, our relationship might not have survived. Our careers were already trying to take priority over our marriage. Our willingness to sacrifice our careers for our relationship helped us to set a lasting priority in our marriage and family.

When we moved to Oregon, I could not find a suitable job for a long time. We lived isolated in the country. I had no friends. I was alone while Barry worked sometimes seventy or more hours a week. For the first time in my life, I confronted my worst enemy—myself. During the long, painful months after moving, I realized how little I actually loved myself. Rather than taking the easy route and getting an outside job, I decided to take on the job of loving myself. I gradually learned how to be happy being by myself. By the end of the year, I was experiencing more joy and fulfillment by just being alone than I had ever felt in any job. My sacrifice for our relationship by moving to Oregon had truly blessed my own heart. In fact, my sacrifice turned out not to be a sacrifice at all! It was, rather, a way of listening to my "still, small voice," which was guiding me to the next step on my spiritual journey.

Is there a sacrifice you need to make to deepen your relationship? If this giving up of personal desire comes from a deep and peaceful place, you will benefit in immeasurable, and often unforeseen, ways.

CONSCIOUS SACRIFICES

Sit quietly by yourself or with a partner.

Reflect on the various times in your life when you have made sacrifices, large and small. Feel if each one was a healthy or unhealthy sacrifice. Did this sacrifice arise from a feeling of guilt? Were you trying to satisfy someone else's expectations? Were you trying to win their love or approval? If you determine that a sacrifice was unhealthy, try to see the negative effects on the relationship. On yourself. On your partner.

Or was this sacrifice made in the spirit of love and giving? If so, can you see the positive effects on the relationship, yourself, and your partner? Can you discover the gifts you have received by making this sacrifice? That you have gained more than you have given up?

19

Relationship Transitions

*Think not you can direct the course of love, for love,
if it finds you worthy, directs your course.*

—KAHLIL GIBRAN

FROM YEARS OF STUDYING RELATIONSHIPS, Joyce and I have come to an important conclusion: *Relationships are never really finished. Once our heart has bonded with someone else's heart, this connection is permanent.* Love is never-ending. We may share a limited duration of togetherness in our lives, but the essence of our togetherness, the love, goes on and on. That's the inspiring news.

On the other hand, the words *separation* or *divorce* invoke painful feelings of failure for many of us. Our society, as well as many others, seems to reinforce that concept of failure. It is not surprising. We live in a world that so glorifies the physical and material side of life in general that relationship is viewed in the same way. Thus, the success of relationships tends to be judged by their physical, or outward, characteristics. Are the partners in the same house? Do they sleep in the same bed? Do they have sex? Do they have children?

We feel, however, that there is only one possible "failure"

regarding your relationships. It has nothing to do with whether you are living together, whether you are married, having "successful" sex, or have a family, or any other outward criteria of success or failure. The one true failure we can experience *is the failure to see the good that is within another human being. It is shutting someone out of your heart.*

Closing your heart to another is really more of a *failing* than a failure, because it is reversible. There is in fact no such thing as permanent failure. We constantly have the choice to open our hearts again. We can more easily do this by realizing that opening our heart to another has nothing to do with living with that person, or even being in their presence at all! It is the inner process that is most important. We open our heart to another when we accept and respect them, when we simply let them be who they are, and bless them on their journey. The truth is, *this person is on the same journey to love as we are.* Their path to love may be different than ours, but we still have the capacity to honor their unique journey.

Many people nowadays have ex-wives or ex-husbands. Most of us have ex-lovers. *If we could just embrace the good that was in each relationship, rather than preoccupying ourselves with only the pain or unhappiness, we could keep alive the heart connection.* If we could be grateful for the valuable spiritual lessons we learned from our past relationships, those lessons could bless our current and future relationships. No matter how bitter your separation or divorce, nor how emotionally distant you feel from a former partner, it's never too late to meditate on the good that was there, or to give thanks for the growth that might not have been possible without that relationship.

TAKING TIME APART

For those currently suffering in a relationship, sometimes the most healing alternative is time apart. The extremity of separation and divorce can sometimes be prevented by consciously taking short time-outs from one another's physical presence. The right use of solitude, allowing space in the relationship, can help a relationship breathe and bring more life back into it. We need to be willing to claim the right amount of alone time that we ourselves need, as well as to be sensitive to our partner's need for solitude. Contrary to what many people believe, needing time alone is not a rejection of our partner. Likewise, when our partner needs space, they are not rejecting us. We need to understand the value of alone time for each partner. When we don't honor either our own or our partner's need for solitude, the relationship will suffer.

I remember a time before we had children when Joyce and I felt particularly stuck. We were having so much difficulty appreciating one another that Joyce asked me to leave for awhile to give her some time alone. We realized each of us was needing some solitude.

I reluctantly packed up our VW van, left Joyce at home, and headed for the mountains a few hours south. We each had complete solitude, which at the time we intuitively knew was important to both of us. Had I gone to stay with a friend, or had Joyce visited with one of her friends, we could have received support, but the company could have also been a distraction from the goal we both held in our hearts. That goal was to see beauty in ourselves, in each other, and in the relationship. We needed to re-envision our connection.

We both worked hard. We meditated and prayed for help. Much of the first day or two, I struggled with numbness and inertia. Joyce struggled with pain and tears. On the third day, a shift occurred. I broke through the inertia and felt peace. With that peace, I could see Joyce in a new light. I could also see that she was human—she had psychological blocks to work through just as I did—but these were her responsibility. Joyce's issues weren't standing in my way or blocking my growth. My issues do that, and sometimes very well indeed.

I saw Joyce as the lover she is, doing and being the best she could, moment by moment. I saw the warmth of her smile, the tenderness of her touch, the innocence of her inner child. I saw her eyes, eyes that saw through me to the depths of my being, eyes that saw what I was feeling even when I didn't know what I was feeling, eyes that caressed me far more tenderly than hands ever could.

Now that I was seeing Joyce and feeling the peace of my soul, I longed to be back with her. Still, rather than immediately jumping into the van and driving home, I spent several more hours deepening my new awareness and peace. I wanted to make it a more permanent part of my consciousness. I wanted to feast rather than nibble.

At the end of the day, I drove down the mountain to the nearest phone booth. I called Joyce and shared with her my feelings and my longing to be back with her. She was ready too. A few hours later, we had a heavenly reunion.

In addition to painful, unplanned separations, Joyce and I have made a conscious effort to be apart, as a planned preventive rather than reactive measure for our growth. These times have benefited our relationship tremendously. During these "retreats" (or better, "advances"), we have used our time alone to bless one another, to visualize the other surrounded in light, to feel how privileged we are to be in this relationship. In our earlier years, we sometimes spent up to a week of solitude to nurture our own souls and bless the relationship. Now, with three children and a busy schedule, we don't have quite the same luxury. But we still need the balancing that comes through time apart. We find a twenty- or thirty-minute meditation in our individual "power spots" can be a sweet dessert in the course of the day. And if, in these intentional times apart, we pray for more love in our marriage, or visualize one another's strength and beauty, then our relationship, as well as our individual lives, are powerfully nourished.

UNRESOLVED RELATIONSHIPS

Often, because of prolonged pain and disharmony in a relationship, one partner decides he or she can't take any more suffering and leaves the relationship. The remaining partner often feels shocked and abandoned, and is often at a loss to understand what has happened.

This was the story of Cass and Daniel. One day, seemingly out of the blue to Daniel, Cass announced she was leaving, packed up, and was gone within hours. They had been having a lot of difficulty in their relationship of late, true, but Daniel felt they were making headway with their problems. While she was packing, he pleaded with Cass to stay and work things out, to go together to a counselor, to go on a vacation together—anything!

After she was gone, Daniel got her phone number from a mutual friend. He felt desperate for some sort of resolution in their relationship, even if it meant this was the end. He wanted to know why she gave up. He called Cass several times. Each time, she refused to talk with him and refused to go with him to a counselor. She told him she did *not* want to work things out with him. She just wanted to be left alone.

So what was Daniel to do? Should he keep pushing for communication and completion? How could he resolve the relationship with Cass unwilling to communicate?

This is not an uncommon situation. In the above example, it was the woman who left. Yet Joyce and I have seen just as many men suddenly leave their partner. And it can happen in new or in long-term relationships.

We tried to show Daniel that he was not, as he believed, an innocent victim. Just because he didn't see or understand his contribution to the situation does not mean he shared no responsibility in the break-up. He still had an equal part in the dance. When Daniel came to us, feeling angry, hurt, and powerless, he was living in denial, ignoring the problems in the relationship, especially his contribution to them. We helped him see that this situation was a mirror for him, that the real source of his suffering was coming from within.

Daniel needed to learn that he was not helpless and powerless in this situation. For him to learn from the mirror, he needed to understand that help must come from within him, rather than from opening communication with Cass. This doesn't mean he needed to stop reaching out to her. We explained that he may need to do a lot more of this, even though he faced rejection and abandonment each time he tried to open this door. His first priority, however, had to be to open the door to his own heart, to establish communication with himself. In this realm, he had full power.

Cass no longer wanting to dance with him didn't mean Daniel was no longer a dancer. *That's because resolution in a relationship does not depend upon both partners. Resolution, like fulfillment, is something that comes from within.* Finding closure is an inner process. Rather than Daniel trying to persuade Cass to come with him to counseling sessions with us, he needed to continue to come by himself to look carefully at his own issues. He needed to look at *his* part of the dance—how he contributed to the disharmony *as well as* how he contributed to the harmony and love he had shared with Cass. When he could see both of these—the light as well as the dark sides of his feelings, the ways he gave his love *and* the ways he withheld it—then resolution would be possible for him whether or not he ever saw Cass again.

But what about Cass? What about a person who simply doesn't want to dance anymore, who doesn't want to communicate or work things out with their partner? She needed a complete sense of distance and time from this relationship. And she also had the same opportunity for resolution as Daniel, if she chose to ask for help. Eventually, she would need to confront all her feelings, just as Daniel did. She might need to return to Daniel's presence, perhaps in a structured setting like counseling, and look more clearly at the difficult issues between them, especially the ways she contributed to them. In other words, she too must look into the mirror of relationship if she wants true resolution, or else she is simply running away from her own issues. If she were to come into Daniel's life, even if only for a discussion, she may need to say some things to him she was unable to say to him when they were together. Again, for her to reach the highest resolution, she would need to feel the love that was there, the love that first drew them together—the love that will always be there, regardless of whether they get back together or stay separate.

RELATIONSHIP HOPPING

When a relationship seems to be "failing," a person may be tempted to hop into another relationship that seems to promise more joy and lightness. Joyce and I received the following letter that illustrates this seductive trap: "There is so much animosity, resentment, even at times hatred in my relationship. I know the love is there, but I feel it so infrequently. Recently I met someone else with whom I feel an attraction and harmony that I can't remember ever feeling in my present relationship. Does this mean I should be with this new person?"

This letter could have come from a man or a woman, in a same-gender or a heterosexual relationship. It really doesn't matter. It's a human instinct to want to leave a difficult relationship. Still, in all honesty, we have to answer "No" to this person's question. For those of you who have been in a similar situation, understand that you can't successfully leave a relationship until you're "finished" with it. Furthermore, you can't fully finish a relationship if you have predominantly negative feelings about your partner. Holding such feelings, you are not free to enter fully into another relationship. If you try, you merely bring all those same feelings with you into the new relationship. We understand the temptation is great to jump right into a new relationship. However, the harmony and attraction you at first feel with a new person will, in time, be marred by the lack of resolution in your present relationship.

We have seen the destructive effects of relationship hopping too many times. We have seen individuals jump from a painful or unfulfilling relationship into another relationship that seemed to hold much more promise. Often, the lure of the new relationship has been the desire for a higher level of clarity, a spiritual connection. Yet, however spiritual and clear a new connection may feel, the unresolved "baggage" from all previous relationships will inevitably pop up.

As we have explained, relationships go through phases. The first or "honeymoon" phase is often blessed with joy and lightness. This is usually due to a lack of ego involvement, an absence of the darker sides of the personalities, which exists in the beginning of most relationships. This early bliss simply cannot last. The complete personalities of both partners must eventually and rightfully make their full entry into the relationship. It is at this time that the lack of closure present in the old relationship will rear its head in the new relationship and demand to be dealt with.

If you want peace and growth with the least possible pain and suffering, *your first priority must be to resolve the problems in the difficult relationship*. And how do you do that? You have two choices. One is to work things out while staying together, and the other is to take time out from the relationship and find clarity in solitude—not with another partner.

Let's look first at the option of staying together. Ask yourself, "Have I done all that I can to heal this relationship?" Obviously, this is not an easy question to answer. It requires deep searching and contemplation. For a relationship to work, there needs to be openness and vulnerability—your own *and* your partner's. Have you sincerely expressed your own need for intimacy and love, or are you more focused on your partner's needs, lacks, and faults? It is far too easy to run away from our own fears and feelings of insecurity, and the easiest way to do this is to project them onto our partner. When we refuse to take responsibility for our own part in the struggles, we thus feel like an unfairly treated victim.

Have you taken the risk of complete honesty with this partner? Do they clearly know what isn't working for you? If you feel they don't hear your spoken words, try writing a heartfelt letter. Remember that any blame, any projection, any attempt at changing this person will most likely be met by resistance or defensiveness. *Vulnerability is your highest honesty*, and it requires that you look into the mirror held up by your partner and discover who you really are in this relationship and what is being reflected back to you. In other words, talk about your own fears, your own pain, your own frustration at not being able to meet your own needs, rather than your partner not being able to meet your needs.

Have you tried seeking outside professional help? A good counselor can help you move past destructive blaming toward self-awareness of your own vulnerability, and help you learn the lessons you are avoiding. Seeing a therapist may be valuable even if your partner does not choose to go with you. Any insights or clarity you receive can benefit your partner. In short, do all that you can to uncover the love that has been buried. Let the vulnerability of your heart guide you always, rather than letting yourself be ruled by your fear and hurt.

If, after a *sincere* effort on your part, your love still remains buried, then it is time to consider the second option. Remember that time apart is not the goal—*clarity is the goal.* Time apart can be a powerful method for healing a relationship only if your intention is focused on this healing, as in the earlier story of my retreat in the mountains. Beware, however: *Time apart can be an escape from your own vulnerability, a way of avoiding the lessons you need to learn.* Since relationship presents us with a looking-glass of our own worst faults, we often run from close-ness as a way of avoiding the pain that is really in us. How will you know if you are running away from yourself? If you are trying to escape, you may find yourself filling your time with all kinds of dis-tractions—places and things as well as people. Most importantly, remember: Becoming intimate with someone else before you are clear with your original partner will usually bring more confusion, more pain, and delay your own process of growth.

How can you make time apart work? We have learned that true solitude can catalyze the fastest growth and thus bring deeper heal-ing to your relationship—*only* if you are willing to do the *inner* work of healing. This means creating enough quality time by yourself, nur-turing your own heart, and uncovering the love that is always there for your partner. The highest mission, however, in your time apart is to find your true best friend, your inner beloved, that radiant being *who is you,* your higher self. Your highest purpose is to connect with this real you.

It is an illusion is that you have "fallen out of love" with another person. In reality, you can only "fall out of love" with yourself. Closing your heart to someone else is a reflection in the mirror show-ing that you are closing your heart to yourself. Once again, feeling our love for another does not necessarily mean we need to spend our life with that person. But the open flow of our love, the honoring of the innate goodness of that person, will give us the clarity and the wisdom to know what to do.

Thus, your relationship will be healed during your time apart as you focus your thoughts and feelings on the good that is there in your partner. This is something that time apart can facilitate. It is often easier to see the beauty and strength of your partner when not in each other's physical presence and environment. Even if your thoughts are flooded with negativity, try to find even the littlest thing to appreciate in your partner, and let it expand from there to include deeper and deeper qualities. *Again, only when your love is flowing will you have the clarity to know whether you need to be together or not.*

After a little time apart, and you have the first breakthrough into tender and caring feelings for your partner, you may experience the temptation to get back together again immediately. Often loneliness is a strong factor, but it is usually a mistake to reunite out of loneliness. It requires real sensitivity and honesty to give the relationship enough time apart so the reunion won't be premature. You may not know your real motive for getting back together. It may perhaps be a deep longing and attraction for your partner. You may not know the real reason until you are physically together. If, after being together for some time, you fall right back into your old patterns of relating, this usually means your reunion was premature. Just give the relationship more time apart, and continue with the inner process of loving.

Relationships need to breathe. Healthy relationships require the balance of time together and time apart. Too much of either will bring imbalance. This is often a difficult lesson for couples to learn, but a vital one if the relationship is to become a true vehicle for transformation and service to the planet.

THE FEAR OF LONELINESS

The desire to find and be with a life partner is profound. So too is the fear of being alone. When our fear of being alone becomes mixed up with our desire to be with our life partner, we lose our clarity and allow the possibility of painful relationship entanglements. Here's an example:

Rhonda felt she had found her life partner, Burt, and then painfully discovered he was married. Despite this, she stayed in a relationship with him for three years. She felt he truly loved her and believed he felt no attraction for his wife but was staying in the marriage only because he loved his children. His decision to stay married was painful for Rhonda because she felt that she and Burt had an important relationship together. She was hurt and longing for a deeper connection when she met Paul. She was thrilled to be with a man whom she described as being completely available to her. Yet, while it was definitely more satisfying to be with a man who was always there for her, she found she couldn't commit herself to Paul while Burt was still so deeply in her heart. Rhonda's pain was becoming unbearable, and she asked us for help.

Pain, whether it is physical or emotional, is a warning signal telling us that something needs to change. Were it not for Rhonda's pain, she might have let these unfulfilling relationships drag on and on. There was no true commitment in either relationship, and commitment is a prerequisite for depth and fulfillment. Rhonda's temptation might have been to cover up or distract herself from the pain she was experiencing, but pain always serves a purpose. If she stays open and aware of this pain, she will eventually feel the action she needs to take.

Let's look at Burt's situation. For Burt to grow, he needs to heal his relationship with his wife. He has most likely projected onto her some of his own negative qualities, and may conveniently assume these are hers alone. He needs to take responsibility for these qualities in himself. For his own growth, he needs to realize that his wife is offering him an opportunity to see himself more clearly. If he does not see his own failure in the marriage and then leaves his wife, these same qualities will most likely be projected onto Rhonda. So, for all his future relationships and his very happiness, it is up to Burt to try as hard as he can to break through to the love he feels for his wife. For love only gets buried, it never dies. Opening his heart to his wife will give Burt the clarity he needs to decide whether or not to leave the marriage.

Burt has a real dilemma. Because of his involvement with Rhonda as well as his wife, he is lacking both true solitude and a deeper sense of himself. His healing depends on his reuniting with himself—a time uninvolved in relationship where he can at last feel who he is, independent of his interaction with women. This can be a scary thing for Burt, for it means letting go of his whole security network— Rhonda *and* his wife. And there are no guarantees for him that either of these two women will be there for him if he ever becomes ready again for relationship. Yet, ironically, if he doesn't let go of both women and take enough time to get to know himself, his security is only a false sense of security. He really has no fulfilling relationship with either woman.

How much alone time is *enough?* It doesn't work to put a time limit on alone time. "Enough" time could be weeks, months, or even years. When Burt gains a sense of himself as a separate person, rather than as enmeshed with a woman, it has then been enough time.

How about Rhonda? Remember what we said earlier about her not distracting herself from the pain of her situation? Clearly, her involvement with a new lover, in this case Paul, is a distraction. With such a deep connection with Burt, and its attendant vulnerability, there is inevitably the fear that Burt will choose his family over Rhonda. Just like Burt and his two women, it is easy to see how a heart that feels insecure in a relationship will gravitate toward protecting itself with a back door—involvement with another person. Again, this is a false protection. The pain and confusion actually increase.

We'd like to offer the same advice for Rhonda that we offered Burt. As long as she is involved in two relationships, she does not have the clarity needed for appropriate action. Rhonda's risk (just like Burt's) is to let go of both relationships long enough to regain a sense of who she is independent of partnership with another.

Letting go is not easy. We are a society largely addicted to relationship. Most people have little sense of self-worth as individuals. Madison Avenue and the media tell us we can't be happy unless we're in a relationship. But *unless we find happiness within first, unless we learn to commune with our own heart and our inner self, how can we be truly happy with another?*

Both Rhonda and Burt are clearly afraid of being alone. They are afraid of the possibility of not being in relationship. As for many people, not to be in relationship is simply not to exist. Many people live by the credo, "I love another, therefore I am." But this is backward logic. The real truth is this: *To discover who I am gives me the capability to love another.* When we overcome our fear of loneliness, our fear of being alone, we learn to appreciate who we are as individuals, and will then draw partners into our life who are available, whole, and willing to offer all of themselves.

When one person begins to take care of themselves, everyone in relationship with that person benefits. Rhonda's separation from both relationships will not only give her the clarity she needs, but will also be a gift to both Burt and Paul. Removing herself from their lives will give an opportunity to all three of them to confront their own issues—to grow in the way they need. Burt can bring peace to his relationship with his wife, whether they stay together or not. Paul can understand more deeply that he had been in a relationship with someone who was unavailable to him. Doing such a thing can inevitably be destructive to his self-worth. Perhaps most important, this time alone will bring a great blessing to Rhonda—if she does her homework. And what is her homework? It is regaining a relationship with herself, romancing herself, nurturing herself, doing those special things that make her happy. It means taking quality time for herself, time for meditation or long walks in nature. It means finding peace in her aloneness and her deeper sense of self.

ENDING BEFORE BEGINNING

Ending a relationship is an important process; it takes time and awareness. Until it is done completely, subsequent new relationships will most likely be confusing and painful. The following is an example:

Leslie and Ken attended one of our couples workshops in the Santa Cruz mountains. They were obviously in love, but looked as if they were carrying a heavy weight. It turned out Leslie had just ended a long-term marriage to be in a new relationship with Ken. All the couples were sitting closely together on the carpet with the majestic redwood trees outside the window, when Leslie shared with us that she had wanted out of her marriage for quite some time, but had lacked the courage to end the relationship until falling in love with Ken. At that moment in the workshop, after several months of blissful romance, the "honeymoon period," Leslie realized with a heavy heart that she could not fully commit to this new relationship with Ken. She realized she was needing time apart from Ken to heal the wounds from her marriage, to bring completion to that relationship. This in turn was causing sadness and frustration for Ken.

Leslie's situation is not unique. It is so typical that people in failing relationships either lack the awareness that the relationship is failing or the courage to heal it or leave it. This awareness and/or courage often only comes in the guise of a new involvement with an outside person. However, the new relationship is off to a poor start because of the unfinished business and lack of closure in the previous relationship.

We suggest some important steps to bring proper completion and closure to a relationship. The first step, as we have emphasized before, is for each partner to create quality time alone—and enough of it. Leslie shared that she had not been without a partner since high school. She really did not have a sense of who she was as an individual. Her whole adult life and identity was wrapped up in her relationships with men. Now she was realizing for the first time that she needed to get to know herself as a separate being—not through the reflection of a lover. She was faced with letting go of the best relationship she felt she ever had with a man, her relationship with Ken.

As we shared before, it takes the willingness to be alone, to say good-bye to an old relationship, to allow real closure. Most people, in that period of aloneness, will experience intense feelings of loneliness. Again, we caution that to involve yourself with a new partner is to sabotage the healing completion that is needed with the original relationship. *Don't be afraid to feel your loneliness.* Many people have told us that they have hardly ever been alone in their life, that they have gone from one relationship to another. We know one woman who only had a *few days* from one relationship to the next from the time she was *sixteen*. And she was now twenty-eight! She said she had no idea who she was as an individual.

It is through experiencing your loneliness and all the feelings that come up through this process, and not pushing these feelings away, that you have a greater opportunity to grow. Confronting your own loneliness can allow you to see the beauty of your partner and discover how much he or she means to you, but, most important, accepting your loneliness will teach you the joy of aloneness ("all-one-ness"). For just on the other side of that loneliness is the fulfillment of really knowing who you are, and therefore knowing your relationship with your own soul.

Leslie planned to take time apart from Ken to achieve closure in her marriage. She understood the risk involved: Ken might not be available when she was finished with this process. She was afraid of this possibility, but knew she needed to face her fear and take this risk.

Step 2 in bringing proper closure to a relationship is constructively processing your upset feelings and the wounds caused by the relationship, including the inevitable feelings of blame and failure that creep in. You can receive valuable help in your solitude through prayer or meditation, but it is often important to seek help from the outside, such as through counseling or supportive groups. Be careful, however, that the help comes from a neutral third party. A friend may not want to confront you with your deeper issues, or may be too much on your side to be neutral.

The final step in completing a relationship is experiencing gratitude. You need to use the time alone to take a careful inventory of the good that was in the relationship. Spend time each day inwardly thanking your former partner for all the positive aspects of your time together. This is an inner process that doesn't depend on any outward communication with this person. Ultimately, however, a person-to-person sharing from the heart or even a letter can bring deep completion.

How do you know when you are ready to be in a new relationship? *You are ready when there is a flow of love from your heart toward your former partner.* This love doesn't depend on that person loving you. In fact, your former partner may still be stuck in hurt, anger, or blame. It isn't even necessary to have personal contact with this person at all. Rather, it is freeing up *your* love that is all important.

Most people are afraid that if they open up to feelings of love for a person they are leaving, they will be tempted to go back into a relationship that is not right for them. On the contrary, it is love that empowers you to do what is right for all involved, no matter how painful it seems on the surface. Take the alone time you need to find that love.

Joyce and I have come to realize that these intimate soul connections called relationships have a destiny of their own. Over the years, we have seen people go through marriage after marriage, divorce after divorce, each relationship bringing new growth and new gifts. We have seen many people learn their soul lessons, peacefully surrender to their aloneness, and then sometimes meet the partner of their dreams, shaking up their entire world. We saw a woman who divorced thirty years ago, had two more divorces, then reunited with her first husband in a relationship that felt new in every way.

The process of my own separations with Joyce has felt like divorce and then remarriage, death, and then rebirth, a completing of a great cycle. All this has given us more trust in a higher plan for our lives, trust in the destiny of relationships. This trust has allowed us to relax more and enjoy the ride of life and of relationship.

If your desire in relationship is to walk side by side on this great journey of life, to grow in love together, to help make this planet a more beautiful place, then you will be brought together with (or brought back together with) the right partner at the most appropriate time—not necessarily the time you desire. So have patience with the unfolding of your life. Embrace the time you are alone, rather than pushing it away. Heal and come to peace with your past relationships. When you can fully celebrate your alone time, and receive the gifts from your past relationships, your heart will be blessed with the greatest joy.

DIVORCE INVOLVING CHILDREN

When children are involved, divorce especially brings a sadness to our mothering and fathering hearts. In our counseling and workshops,

Barry and I see many couples who are on the brink of separating. We try hard to point out the possibility for healing and growth. Sometimes, as we did with Rhonda and Burt, we recommend time apart or retreat time when the wounds or resentment are just too great.

Divorce, especially in families with children, is not to be taken lightly. Not only will the divorce affect the lives of the parents, but it will also dramatically affect the lives of each of the children. We often hear adults describe to us the saddest day of their childhood as the day their parents told them they were getting a divorce. Most can describe in striking and poignant detail everything that was said and done that particular day.

Children come to both parents, so they naturally desire to have the family stay together. Long after the divorce, children will still try to devise in their minds and hearts a way to bring their parents back together. A parent might find a more loving connection with another partner. In a child's heart, however, there can be no replacement for their own absent parent.

Divorce can have unforeseen repercussions far beyond the original pain of loss. Through divorce, you are taking away from your children the model of a committed relationship that will endure the test of love. When your children are adults and have difficulty in their own relationships, they will tend to follow your example.

Perhaps we are painting a rather dismal picture, but we often see adults choosing the easy route in relationship, thinking about their own happiness and attractions while failing to consider deeply the lifelong effect on their children. When your mind starts thinking of divorce as a way out of your problems with your partner, we recommend that you stop for a moment. First, picture each of your children and feel how much they love and need the other parent. Then ask yourself, "Is there anything else I can do for this relationship? Could I forgive more or be more open? Could I try more appreciation rather than criticism? Have I been praying and asking enough for help? Could I look deeper and see this person's higher self? Have I been truly honest? Have I had the courage to say 'No' when I really needed to?"

Sometimes we resist working more on our relationship, especially when we *perceive* our partner as not working as much as we are. This attitude is self-defeating; remember, every time we try to love and forgive, we are really doing it for ourselves, not for our partner. We have come to Earth to grow and learn. Often, these painful experiences in relationship catalyze our deepest growth and expansion. Rather than concentrating on the ways your partner is ruining the relationship, try to see what is reflected in the mirror of your lover's eyes and concentrate on the ways *you* could try harder. We're not advocating codependence, that you take responsibility for your partner. Neither are we recommending burying your head in the sand of denial. But we are rather urging you to go the extra distance and learn your own lessons.

When I was thirteen, my mother and I were driving home from grocery shopping. We were stopped in the left turn lane. My mother suddenly turned to me and said, "I'm thinking of leaving your father."

I remember every detail of the experience. I felt totally sick inside.

"Then I will go and live with Aunt Almeda, because I won't choose one or the other of you," I said emphatically.

My mother later told me that my comment shook up her whole world. She realized that she could lose *me* as well as her husband through a divorce. She tried harder in the relationship. My father tried harder, too. Soon the wound was healing and they were genuinely enjoying each other again.

Both Barry's and my parents have been married for over fifty years. Now in their later years, our parents are deeply devoted to one another. As children, Barry and I both watched our parents struggle and also find the strength to overcome their obstacles. Our parents have been powerful models for us and have helped us by example many times when we felt like giving up on each other.

Suppose you have done all you can do and still there are barriers you and your partner cannot overcome. Drug or alcohol abuse can be one such barrier. So can other addictive or compulsive behaviors, or physical or emotional abuse, or violence. You know in your heart that you must separate and you have also deeply considered the effect upon your children. What now? Remember, no matter how difficult the relationship is with your partner, *your children still love and need connection with both their mother and their father.* That bond of love must be tenderly sheltered by you during all the events leading up to and after the separation. *All children deserve the right to continue to cherish and honor both of their parents.* If you have a negative feeling toward their other parent, it needs to be vented in an appropriate setting, *not to your children.*

In your own heart, you can still seek to love and honor your partner, even if you feel you must separate from them. The model of a family that stays together will be taken away from your children, but you can offer them another important model for life, *the model of a parent who refused to shut someone out of their heart.* You can offer your child the model of a parent who kept on loving after divorce and respected the tender bond between a child and *both* parents. This model will have a powerful impact on your child's life.

20

Refilling the Cup of Love

*I see the truth in thee, and what is in thee is in me,
and I am that I am.*

—UPANISHADS

ARRY AND I RECEIVED THE FOLLOWING LETTER THAT SPEAKS so well to the struggles people experience in their relationships that it could have come from almost any couple: "Our love and attraction was strong in the beginning of our relationship. Now we seem to have lost the connection. We want to save our relationship, but are losing faith. Do you feel it is possible for a couple to find love again?"

First of all, it is important for couples to understand that their love and attraction for one another is never lost. *Once there has been a deep love and connection between two people, this love exists for all time.* When two people dwell in the feeling of pure love, which often happens in the beginning of a relationship, both hearts are opened and it feels as if the cup of love that flows between them is full. A mistake new lovers can make is to assume the cup of love will always be filled without their recognizing and acknowledging from where this divine nectar comes. The couple drinks from the cup, but unless they consciously remember to fill it again, it eventually runs dry. Then they feel as if the love is gone. They forget they are still holding onto the cup, which always exists between them and can be refilled to overflowing. So the real question is not whether a couple can find love again, but whether they want to fill their cup once more, *and* whether they are willing to do what may be necessary.

At this point in a relationship, many people are tempted to look to their partner to refill the cup of love. It may be obvious how the other person is not being loving enough. This attitude, however, ignores the mirror of relationship, and will surely fail.

The most powerful way to refill your cup of love and to keep it filled is to remember the source of that love, to remember your love is a gift from the heart of the universe, a gift from God. Go right to that source and ask that your cup be refilled, your relationship strengthened, your love be made strong and whole once again. You will be shown the way. All you need to do is sincerely ask.

Barry and I often pray together to ask for strength, clarity, and deeper love and understanding in our relationship. Our prayer also expresses our gratitude and asks that we be allowed to continue to help on this Earth. When I hear Barry's prayer, I am always touched by the sincerity of his words. This spoken sincerity allows me to understand more fully his inner nature. I always feel closer to Barry after we pray together.

At our couples' retreats, we always ask the couples to pray together toward the end of our time. We feel that the most important reminder we can give couples is to go inside to their source for help and inspiration. Asking and wanting to receive God's presence into your relationship is a powerful way to grow closer in love and understanding. Acknowledging that you each have the same source, the same great light within, brings a comfort and peace to your relationship. And remember, you don't have to have the same religious practice to pray together—two people can be of different religions and yet they can still pray to the same source of love.

At a recent couples' workshop, one couple was having a hard time in their relationship. Coming to the weekend was a final attempt to save their twelve-year marriage. They had gone to several marriage counselors without much success. We noticed the man was particularly resistant to every practice and process we had the participants do. He often sat in the back of the room, arms folded across his chest, looking bored. Finally, at the end of the morning meditation on the last day, we had the couples sit and pray together. Reluctantly, this man bent his head towards his wife. They prayed together for the first time in their relationship, each asking for help to save their marriage. After they had prayed and listened to each other's prayers, the dam holding back the reservoir crumbled, and tears started flowing. Their hearts had finally opened to one another. This couple still has a distance to go to fill their cup of love, for they had let it run dry long ago. But their prayer brought in the first drops of nectar and, with it, hope and inspiration for their future.

Prayer is a powerful way to bring greater harmony into our relationships. We are all sometimes confronted by barriers or blocks that seem to keep us from loving each other as fully as we could. Of course, it is important to talk with one another. However, sometimes the talking over problems can be overdone, making us feel even more stuck. It is at times like these that the couple can put their heads together and pray, asking that God, the Omnipresent Spirit of Love, give them fresh insight and clarity. Asking friends or a group to pray with us can make the experience even more powerful. Through our willingness to ask for help, and our humility, we can become receptive to a higher wisdom.

PARTNERS IN PRAYER

Sit facing one another and bow your heads together so your foreheads touch. You can each acknowledge your source of love and light and remember it is the desire of your Creator that you both know love. Then simply pray, taking turns speaking words from your heart, loud enough so your partner can hear. Ask for what you need, such as help and guidance, and give thanks for all that has been given to you.

Next, let there be a time of silence in which you receive. This is when the divine nectar can again flow into your cup. It may come in the form of pure energy, inspiration, or guidance, such as ways to forgive, overcome obstacles, or appreciate someone or something. Much strength can come from a regular habit of praying together and acknowledging the source of our love.

Another powerful way to refill our cup of love is to be in nature. Relationships can benefit greatly from the healing contact with the Earth and its wealth. Connecting with nature is like a prayer in itself. It is all too easy for most of us to get caught up in the busy-ness of the world—making money, keeping appointments, and returning all the calls on our answering machines can become the main focus of life. Our relationships can easily take a back seat, but being in nature and getting closer to the Earth has a powerful way of helping us set priorities and regain our connection. We have found in our own relationship that nature has always served as one of our greatest healers.

In 1972, when we were living in Los Angeles, we had been bitterly separated for a week and felt little hope of ever continuing the relationship. The hurt and pain were deeply entrenched. After much hesitation, we decided to take a hike along our favorite trail in the mountains. The drive there was difficult, with a prevailing tone of anger and resentment. We decided to take the hike in silence and concentrate on the surroundings rather than trying to communicate verbally.

The first half mile, we stomped along, kicking stones and pine cones as we went. Then we both noticed our footsteps softened and the need to kick stones disappeared. The thoughts of anger and separation faded and were replaced by our appreciation of this beautiful trail.

After several hours, we stopped to rest by a tree. We were able to look at each other without anger for the first time in what seemed like an eternity. We walked on and came to a beautiful meadow filled with orange and yellow wildflowers. We laid down to rest in the sun and soon fell asleep. When we awoke, we looked at each other, kissed, and hugged. The physical contact felt wonderfully good after the long period of isolation. It was as if our bodies were trying to say, "Forget those thoughts and grudges. Listen to *our* needs for touch and closeness."

We looked deeply into each other's eyes. Nature had helped lift the veil of separation and revealed our union. We still had a big challenge, with years of work ahead of us to clear the anger and resentment, and to learn to trust once again. Still, Mother Nature had helped us to recapture the vision of our original wholeness and commitment to love, which then inspired us to continue with the healing of our relationship.

We now try to be in nature as often as possible. We know through continuing contact with the Earth, trees, rivers, ocean, and lakes, we are restored and inspired.

Jeffrey Golitz has written a book entitled *The Secret Life of Trees* in which he explains how trees give off energy that benefits human beings. Perhaps, rather than sitting in your living room, it would be to your advantage to walk among the trees and receive the healing gift of nature. Spending time in nature can heal the human heart, set the highest priorities, and help restore union and vision.

RECEIVING NATURE'S GIFTS

Plan a full day to be in nature, either alone or with your partner. Pack a lunch and whatever else you need, and hike away from civilization and people. Find a quiet, isolated place of beauty—a power spot. Sit or lie on the ground and be still. Allow the healing energies of nature to flow into your body. Listen and feel.... Give your mind a rest from the many thoughts, problems, and plans of your life. This is a time to be quiet and receive the gifts nature has to give you.

When you are ready to leave, thank the Earth and all of nature for helping you.

RENEWING RELATIONSHIPS

A powerful and effective way to nurture a relationship is to constantly bring newness into it. Love in a relationship gets buried when life together becomes a boring routine. Our souls need freshness, enthusiasm, and newness to keep growing. Evolution is a spiritual need of every person. Bringing newness and growth to our own souls will bless our relationship. Bringing fresh air into our relationship will bless our own spiritual evolution. When we grow as individuals, our relationship grows. And when our relationship grows, we grow as individuals.

In May 1992, we hired a baby-sitter for a day to watch our two younger children for twelve hours. At the time, we didn't usually leave three-year-old John-Nuriel for that long unless we were out of town working, but we felt we needed to rejuvenate our relationship. The demands of building our own home and center, as well as all the usual work of counseling, workshops, taking care of the children, and running our publishing company had become exhausting, and we found ourselves too often relating in a superficial, businesslike way.

We drove to the Big Sur coast, parked our car and walked two miles to a secluded beach. We were enjoying our lunch in solitude when we looked up and saw a troop of Boy Scouts coming down the cliff trail. Soon the beach was filled with thirty young Scouts yelling and screaming. All sense of privacy was lost.

Barry pointed to the end of the beach, a rocky point with waves crashing against the rocks. "It's tricky," he said with a twinkle in his eye, "but I know how to cross that point." I knew that Barry, being adventurous, had crossed it several times before. I tend to follow a safe and easy route, but we had devoted this day to bringing newness into our relationship. I took off my hiking shoes and said, "I'll trust you, let's go!"

For the next half-hour, we braved rocky cliffs and waves. At one point, we clung to a rock while cold water splashed over our heads. After the cold and wet ordeal, a most beautiful scene stretched out before us. We were all alone on a half-mile stretch of wilderness beach. We took off our clothes and warmed our naked bodies. We played and danced and made love in the sun. Each of us felt transported to a new realm. The experience was romantic, inspiring, and expanding, letting us feel our own and each other's magical essence. We stayed in that heavenly physical and spiritual place for hours, then hiked out in the sunset.

The next day, there were the same stresses with house-building, business, and family. We entered fully into the work. At times, we got caught up again in the hectic activities, but then we remembered our experience on the beach, took time to hug and kiss, and to allow the deeper part of our being to emerge. Our day together had reminded us of the ever-new joy in our relationship—and the possibility of bringing that joy into the busiest of days.

Newness comes in many forms. The most important prerequisite is a willingness to grow and expand together. Taking part in a couples' weekend workshop or ongoing couples' support group is an excellent way to change and become inspired together. Or a couple may choose to work together on a new and interesting project that will help others. Helping others tends to strengthen and uplift a relationship. Taking up a hobby together can also add interest and growth. For some people, there is gardening or hiking. For the more adventurous, there is skydiving or whitewater rafting. It doesn't matter what you do. Even everyday activities, such as a shared trip to the grocery store, and then creating a way to make it more fun, can turn into a new way to be together and can help to renew your love.

My parents, Louise and Henry, are now seventy-eight and eighty-four years old. A part of their lives is spent in the routine of weekly blood tests and visits to the doctor. My dad has almost completely lost his hearing, making conversation with my mother limited. Despite their own physical limitations, these two decided to do something challenging together. Every week they help prepare a meal for fourteen homeless men. They go to their church to serve the food and offer encouragement and hope. To many of these men, my mother and father are like the loving family they wish they had had. Their gratitude and love for my parents is constantly present. For my parents, this act of giving to others brings newness and inspiration into their lives and relationship.

Barry's parents, Helen and Michael, are both in their late seventies. As with my parents, physical ailments necessitate frequent medical visits. Yet just when the rest of the family is thinking Grandma and Grandpa won't be able to do anything but stay in their mobile home and rest, they announce they are taking a cruise. Some of us may protest, "But what about your diabetes? What about your bad heart?" They always respond in the same way, "We still want to have fun!" The cruises, the trips, the adventures all bring a sense of newness and joy into their lives that is immediately translated into their relationship.

In 1974, we decided not to have children. We simply felt our lives would change too much, and we were content. After eleven years, we had finally come to a place where our relationship was easy. We'd reached one of those plateaus of growth where we felt we wanted a rest. We had learned how to communicate more effectively, how to give each other freedom. We were meditating long periods each day and feeling peaceful. We were convinced a child would interrupt our peace.

A spiritual teacher who was living near us, Baba Hari Dass, helped us the most in this area. Each time he saw us he asked, "When are you going to have children?" Each time, we patiently explained that we didn't want to change our lives by inviting a child to join us. Finally, he had heard enough of our excuses and wisely replied, "The nature of life is change. You can't stop it."

A month later, we took the risk, and I became pregnant. Nine months later, I gave birth at home to a beautiful baby girl. Our children, Rami, Mira, and John-Nuriel, have changed our lives and our relationship in very positive ways. Instead of meditating long periods and concentrating so totally on our relationship, we have been graced with ever-widening, humble, and grateful hearts. Through loving the children, our love for each other has expanded as well.

Seek ways to bring newness into your relationship. Sometimes it takes a risk to step out of your ordinary routines. Do something different together and watch your relationship expand and grow.

21

The Path
of Service

The surest way to live with honor in the world is to be in reality what we appear to be.

—SOCRATES

A S WE EXPLAINED IN CHAPTER 1, WE LIKE TO VIEW the relationship journey as having three phases, comparable to the phases of spiritual growth. The first phase is the "heavenly glimpse," the falling (or better, rising) in love, the opening wide of hearts. This is the "honeymoon" phase, the taste of unconditional love that whets the appetite for more of this nectar.

The second phase of the relationship journey is the uniting of both lovers into a solid connection, the working through of issues that stand in the way of love, the establishing of a true commitment to love and to one another. Each difficulty that is overcome, each dark night that finds its way to a bright new dawn, each angry thought that a lover transforms into a kind and gentle thought, is a step toward unconditional loving.

The third phase is service, the offering of the union as a gift to the world, the willingness to share the fruits of the relationship with others. Couples can easily get stuck in phase 2, in the process of working things out in the relationship, and the excitement of learning many lessons. But it is important to our spiritual growth that we reach phase 3. I remember toward the end of our two years of travel and spiritual study, Joyce and I visited an older woman who asked us what we were doing with our lives. We told her about our voyage of discovery, and how much we were learning about ourselves and our relationship. She asked quite clearly, "But what are you doing for others?"

"All that can wait," I said. "Right now, there's so much to discover and learn."

She looked at us sadly and said, "You two are like the Dead Sea. Rivers flow into it, but nothing flows out of it. Because of that, nothing can live in its waters. It's stagnant, dead."

We realized the truth in her words. We needed to teach others what we had learned, to love others in the ways we had been loved, to give the gifts that we had come here on Earth to give. Through serving others, the waters of our internal sea could find an outlet, and could come to life.

As we have contemplated the nature of service we've come to see that it has an inner and an outer aspect.

INNER SERVICE

Once a couple is joined together in their hearts, their union is in itself a gift to the world. In truth, we feel every time two people break through the barriers of the ego and learn to love one another, that in itself is an act of service to the world. For love is like a perfume that makes the world a little more fragrant.

Not long ago, at a weekend retreat, Joyce and I shared with a group of couples our desire to have time away from home, office, and children—time to be alone in nature to devote to loving one another. In front of these couples, we made a vow to do this once a week, no matter how busy we were. A woman sitting close to us took our hands in hers as if to make sure her message would be received by us. She said clearly and powerfully, "Many people depend on you two taking this time to nourish your relationship."

She was right, and Joyce and I needed to hear this truth. Even after all these years together, we still needed to set aside quality time to be alone and to cultivate our love. And this time of loving one another had a farther-reaching effect than either of us was willing to acknowledge. We needed to accept that we are serving others through opening our hearts to one another, and therefore replenishing the love in our own relationship is replenishing the love in the world. And we know this applies to all couples.

Inner service relates to *being* rather than doing. Who we are as individuals, couples, and families speaks louder than what we do. We have recognized this truth for a long time. In our workshops and retreats, people have always told us they learned more from the example of who we are as a relationship or family than what we taught by our words. One couple told us they had received the most by not listening to anything we said. Instead, they watched us as they would watch a TV with no sound. They watched our hand movements, the expressions on our faces, the ways we looked at each other. They noticed all the little ways we loved and respected each other, as well as the ways we worked things out, deciding as an intimate partnership who would say what, and when each of us would speak. We like to think what we have to say is also worthwhile, but we truly appreciated how this couple saw us. Joyce and I do the same thing with couples we admire.

OUTER SERVICE

Yet this inner service is not enough. For our relationships to become fulfilled in the highest way, we must find a way to help others. *Being* in love is fundamental, but *doing* love is also necessary. This is *outer service*, which includes such things as reaching out to a friend in need, spending time with the children of a single parent, cleaning the house of someone who is ill, or other acts of helping.

As we do such outer service, we need always to remember it is not *what* we do but *how* we do it that is important. Mother Teresa liked to say, "Little things done for the love of God become big things." When our motivation for service is simply to help, rather than to *get* recognition or anything else, every act of service is important.

Every relationship needs enough quality time of togetherness to keep the love flowing. Likewise, every couple needs quality time of serving together for spiritual fulfillment. Quality, rather than quantity, is the important factor. We know a couple who volunteered one evening a week in a soup kitchen feeding the homeless. This service project fed them as a couple just as much as it fed the people. They grew to look forward to these evenings because of the joy it gave them to give their love to others.

Of course, there is joy in giving and serving as an individual. To do so as a couple, however, sharing this service side by side, unites that couple in a deeper way. We have seen couples who were stuck in their relationship become unstuck through the process of helping others. When people come to Joyce and me for help, we are amazed at how often their issues are our issues. Helping them with their problems gives us insight into our own. Giving our love and help to others seems to have a "boomerang effect." It comes right back to us, allowing more love and healing in our own relationship.

Service can take many different forms. A couple's shared service can also be their shared creativity. Being creative together is giving a unique gift to the world. A couple we knew, Jenny and Ted, held in their hearts for many years the vision of singing together. They felt they weren't good enough and became proficient at making excuses. Their hearts, however, were full to overflowing with the gift of music and song. Finally they pushed past their insecurities and started recording a tape. Shortly before it was finished, Ted died quite suddenly and tragically. Musically talented friends all rallied together and helped finish the tape.

Jenny's grief was profound. However, even the start of giving their shared gift to the world has helped her in her grieving and blessed her in her continued service. Imagine how much greater her grief might have been if they had done nothing about their inspiration.

Creating and raising a loving family is also a powerful act of service. Nurturing your children and supporting them in their growth blesses many more people than just your own family. Every drop of love and caring you give to children, whether yours or someone else's, is directly helping the future of this world.

There is an urgent need in the world today for examples of loving relationship and family. Couples who work together to serve others, to make the world a more beautiful place, to manifest their own unique vision of love, are giving the world a model of a holy relationship and a truly functional family.

SERVING TOGETHER

Is there some way, no matter how small, that you and a loved one can serve together? Is there a way you can both help make this planet a better place? A more beautiful place?

Remember, service can be helping others as well as creating more beauty. Also remember, serving together is a way to enrich your own relationship. Don't put it off.

22

Love Is Forever

Lord, you are my lover, my longing, my flowing stream, my sun, and I am your reflection.

—MECHTILD OF MAGDEBURG

ONE FUNDAMENTAL TRUTH SEEMS CENTRAL to most spiritual traditions: We human beings are more than our physical bodies, minds, and emotions. We have a deeper, more essential nature that transcends time and space. Depending upon the tradition, this part of us is called the soul, the psyche, the heart, the light body, the Self, or many other terms. Love, the most powerful force for good, emanates from this deeper place. In addition, because love comes from a part of us that is eternal, love itself is eternal. Death cannot bring an end to love. In my deepest place of knowing, I feel I will always be with Barry and he with me.

To learn the truth of that, many years ago Barry and I started an exercise we call "practicing the presence of one another." We share it here.

PRACTICING ONE ANOTHER'S PRESENCE

Go off by yourself so you are totally separate from someone you love, or wait for a time when you are alone.

Close your eyes and visualize this beloved. Especially try to feel who this person really is. Feel your gratitude and appreciation for all the good they have brought into your life. Feel the qualities of their soul that have enriched your life. Open your heart to the preciousness of your shared love.

In this feeling of love and connection, ask yourself, "Where can my beloved go?" Try to see how this union of two hearts is lasting. Death cannot separate your soul from your beloved. The physical relationship may change, but not the union of your hearts.

Barry and I have practiced this exercise for most of our marriage. It is becoming clear to us that we can never really be separated. Our love for one another is forever. We feel that constantly practicing this exercise in each other's physical absence will help us when death does come to one of us. We each hope to practice this exercise for the duration of our time on Earth.

The eventual death of a loved one is inevitable and unavoidable. Bringing this reality into consciousness will benefit both partners. To pretend that death will never happen to you or to your partner is to live in denial, thus making real depth and commitment difficult. At the same time, to live in fear or to harbor a morbid preoccupation with the idea of your partner dying can block the creative, life-giving energies of a relationship. The possibility of death needs to be made conscious, needs to be talked about with sensitivity and openness. Opening to the possibility of death can bring a couple much closer to one another and allow them to be more mutually appreciative.

Elisabeth Kübler-Ross talks about the "little deaths" that prepare us for the "big death," the death of our body and of our loved ones. She advises us to bring more awareness and acceptance into these little deaths, the losses we are constantly experiencing all throughout life. Every loss we can meet with an open heart is preparing us to greet death with an open heart. In our relationships, we can prepare for the loss of a partner by practicing bringing more heart and openness to the little, day-to-day losses.

Some years ago, Barry and I were leading a retreat in Hawaii. The week was going smoothly, more smoothly than any other retreat. The people were open, enthusiastic, and loving. The weather was perfect, the food was great. Everything was going so perfectly, it felt as if we were all getting ready for something important. Then something did happen that deeply affected us all. Our group was notified that a man was lost in an underground lava tube. The man, Richard, was not a part of our group but was a guest of the retreat center where we were staying. He and his wife, Karen, had entered one of the local steam vents that are used by the Hawaiians for ceremonies. Karen became too hot and left Richard in the sauna-like cave with a friend. She waited for him outside. Richard never came out. While he was following the friend out of the tube, Richard somehow turned off into a side chamber. Several hours later, his body was found. He had died, probably from hyperthermia and lack of oxygen.

Our whole group felt saddened by the news, and our hearts went out to Karen. We told the retreat center staff we would like to help in any way we could. The next morning, they told us Richard's widow of only fourteen hours would be joining our group for meditation. We didn't know what to expect. Was she open to the spiritual dimension of life that we were teaching? Would she be receptive to our support?

As it turned out, Karen had read our books and felt deeply sympathetic toward our work. That morning, we provided a safe and nurturing place for Karen to begin the process of grieving, as well as opening to connect with Richard in a new way. She stayed an integral part of our group for two days, and we supported her while her husband's body was cremated.

But Karen gave even more to us! With incredible wisdom, clarity, and depth, she told our group, "*You may never know when the time will come for a loved one to die. Don't ever assume you will be together in these bodies for a long time. Don't take each other for granted. Now is the time to appreciate and express your love to one another.*"

Karen explained how she and Richard had meditated together for over ten years. They were so close that they were constantly reading each other's thoughts. Because of this deep soul attunement, they always assumed they would know if one of them were going to die. Yet in the last several days before Richard's death, Karen was unable to read his thoughts, unable to have that sensitive and deep connection with him. She felt she was somehow blocked from knowing of his approaching death. So it was a complete surprise to her. Ordinarily, she would have tried to prevent Richard from going into such a potentially dangerous place, but his determination was so clear that she offered no resistance.

Time after time, Karen looked deeply at our group and urged, "You just never know. Don't waste a single moment. Don't put off loving until tomorrow." It was a theme that permeated the atmosphere of the rest of the retreat and is living on in each day of our lives now.

Staying aware of the possibility of death can help you feel a steady flow of appreciation and gratitude for your partner. If you knew your partner was going to die tomorrow, would you waste another minute ignoring them or taking them for granted? Of course not! Since we do not know the time of a loved one's death, now is the time to appreciate and feel grateful.

Two days before Richard's death, Barry and I had hosted an evening open-house, inviting people from the local community and guests of the retreat center. Richard and Karen had come. We had done one of our favorite things: an exercise in which people paired up and spoke words of gratitude and appreciation to one another. Karen told us she and Richard appreciated each other more deeply than they ever had. They spoke to one another with words of tender love. At the end of the exercise, someone noticed how happy they looked and snapped a picture of them. The picture is now a constant reminder to Karen of their final vows of love and gratitude. Those words of appreciation are among her treasured memories.

We have seen people try to protect themselves from the pain of death by keeping their distance from their partner. They figure if they never *fully love* their partner, then the death of that person will not be so devastating. However, this approach to loss causes even more pain. A person who is grieving the loss of a loved one does not grieve over how much love they gave to their beloved. Instead, they grieve over the ways they didn't fully express their love. When you have loved your partner fully, it is easier to grieve their absence than when you have spent energy protecting yourself against the loss. Now is the time to love fully, knowing this is the only real protection.

In the touching ending of the movie *Ghost*, Molly's dead lover, Sam, has been trying in vain to find a way through the curtain of death, partly to protect his beloved but also to let her know he is still with her. Finally the curtain between the two worlds parts and she can see him. His message is worth remembering: *"Molly, it's amazing! The love inside—you get to take it with you."*

MOMENTS OF RECKONING

I recently had a moment in my life that seemed to test me to the very core of my being. My parents had sold their home on the East Coast a few years ago so they could live next door to our family in our guest house for six months each year, and close to my brother in Minnesota the other six months. On the afternoon of, April 3, 1994 Easter Sunday, my mother rushed over, calling for help. Something was wrong with my dad. Barry and I ran back to the guest house. We quickly realized the seriousness of the situation. My eighty-two-year-old father, who had always been active and independent, was suddenly close to death. His face was an ashen gray color, his breathing extremely labored. Barry did all that he could medically while my mother called 911. I sat holding my dad's hand. Without any warning, the moment of death seemed to be upon him. He knew it and I knew it. I looked into his eyes for what I thought would be the last time.

"I love you, Dad." Unable to speak and gasping for air, he still winked back. It was just a moment, a few seconds in time, yet those few seconds tested me to the core. I needed to access instantly all the work I had done on forgiving, letting go, and accepting my father. In that moment, I felt how much I loved my father, and I felt a deep gratitude for having been able to express this love over the years. Though shocked by the suddenness of the moment, I was grateful for the power of love that surged through me for my father. If I never saw him again, I knew that love had flowed between us in this moment. The mistakes, the misunderstandings, the failures to communicate were all forgiven. There was only love now.

The paramedics soon arrived and administered oxygen. A large blood clot in his lungs had possibly come within minutes of taking my father's life. We rushed him to the hospital. His condition was critical, but he was going to make it.

I have long reflected on that moment of near death. It was totally unexpected, and yet it entered our lives with tremendous power. When a moment like that comes, it cannot be ignored. How often do we live our everyday lives ignoring the possibility of these moments? A harsh word is spoken to a loved one and we hang up the phone. Anger is left unresolved. An inner prompting to reach out is ignored. Due to discomfort, neglect, or hurry, love goes unexpressed. And yet the moment of death of a loved one can come so quickly and catch us unaware. We simply cannot take the risk of letting anger go unresolved or ignore the prompting to love. The time is now. Bereavement counselors share that the memory of expressed love brings comfort, while the memory of unresolved or unexpressed feelings brings sorrow. Now is the time to reach out and express your caring and love. None of us can take the chance and wait.

Is there a call you need to make or a letter you need to write today? Is there a hug or an appreciation you need to give? Do it now! You will never regret the outpouring of love.

23

Completing Our Assignment

To laugh is to risk appearing foolish.
To weep is to risk appearing sentimental.
To reach out for another is to risk involvement.
To expose feelings is to risk exposing your true self.
To hope is to risk despair.
To try is to risk failure.
To live is to risk dying.

—Anonymous

It is tempting to want a vacation from life's challenges—a vacation from growth itself. Maybe you had been single a long time and are now finally in a relationship. You can see the problem areas you need to work on, but why rock the boat? Maybe you are married and can see plenty of ways to become more deeply connected with both yourself and your partner, but why make waves?

Years ago, when Joyce and I were just starting an intense two-year period of closeness (counseling, really) with Ram Dass, he told us something quite profound—and a bit scary. He said, "You've come to me with a tidy cart filled with neatly arranged apples. I'm going to help you dump the cart and spill the apples all over the place."

In time, we came to understand what he meant. We learned that the apples on the top of our cart were the large, polished, prettiest ones, pleasing to the eyes. Just underneath were the smaller, misshapen apples, not as pleasing to some eyes, but every bit as good and important.

We human beings learn quickly in life how to cover up the darker sides of our personalities, the imperfect apples. We learn how to create an outward appearance or image that is more acceptable to others. The sorrow of not being seen and understood as little children was too much to bear, so we learned to hide our deeper feelings.

Now, however, this false image is working against us. It is keeping us enclosed in a shell, a prison of locked-in feelings. For real growth, we need to embrace all of ourselves, our tender and vulnerable feelings, our pain, sorrow, fear, and anger, our playfulness, joy, strength, and love—every part of our being. Each feeling, each aspect of our personality, has its own uniqueness, goodness, and beauty.

So how do we grow to understand ourselves? We do this by taking risks in our lives. We do this by living fully moment by moment. This is living from the heart. Helen Keller once said, "Life is a daring adventure, or nothing at all!"

In my relationship with Joyce, I risked when I decided to get married, taking a leap of faith into commitment. I risk every time I share my vulnerable feelings with her, when my ego self would have me remain closed and "protected." I also risk when I give myself quality quiet time to feel my love and gratitude for life, because in these times, my mind often runs rampant. My risk is to persist quietly in my meditation, until my disjointed thoughts are replaced with peace, and in that peace, my heart fills up with love and gratitude.

So what keeps us from our highest spiritual growth? Our fear and our feelings of unworthiness. We feel unworthy to live our lives with our full loving potential. We've been told or have told ourselves that we're *bad* boys and girls, so we don't deserve to live in love, except maybe for a brief moment.

Rather than dwelling on these unworthy feelings, imagine for a moment that you were not simply born into your family in a random, haphazard way. Imagine that you came here on a definite mission, with a clear assignment and specific purpose. Joyce and I feel each person comes into this world to complete an important assignment: *to learn to love and be loved in the fullest possible way.* We don't have to settle for a little love, a superficially comfortable relationship, a busy life filled with "important" material goals—a neat and tidy apple cart. One of our favorite songs, written by our friend, John Astin, puts it simply:

> *Why have you come to earth?*
> *Do you remember?*
> *Why have you taken birth?*
> *Why have you come?*
> *To love ... serve ... and remember.*

All of us came here to discover the many facets of ourselves. We came here to make this world a better place, to give the gifts that only we can give, because each one of us is unique. To allow our relationships to reach their highest potential is to give a powerful gift to the world.

We came here to remember who we really are, to discover ourselves as souls far deeper than our bodies and personalities. We are lovers, beings of radiant luminosity, Gods and Goddesses sharing the substance and intelligence of life with all of creation. We are creator and creation, giver and receiver of love, divine as well as human beings.

When I take the time to look deeply into Joyce's eyes, I can see a face behind her face. It is as if her outer face becomes somewhat translucent, and I can see what is deeper. It is the same face every time. It has never aged. It remains youthful, softly suffused with light, magnificent in its beauty, and deeply peaceful. I recognize this face as the *real* Joyce. What is more challenging is to recognize that I am also looking into a mirror, reflecting back an image of my own eternal face and being. If, in those magical moments, Joyce is a divine Goddess, than I must be a divine God.

I know this to be true. It is just so wonderful to behold the Goddess outside of myself that I can become entranced with her beauty. I sometimes need to almost shake myself from this trance, so I can feel who is seeing all this beauty. *The one who sees is the God of me.* Perhaps the highest work I ever do on myself is to break this outward trance, and focus *inside* on the divine being who sees only goodness and beauty. Then I am taking responsibility for being a soul mirror rather than just looking into one. And I can see that this Goddess in front of me is beholding a God. I see her looking into the mirror of my heart. Together, we are a balance of wholeness.

We each have an awesome privilege of bringing out this God or Goddess in one another. Beholding such exquisite beauty in each other gives that beauty reality, brings it to the surface. Appreciating what we see with the spoken or written word is to honor this beauty, which also draws it forth. Letting ourself be seen by our beloved, making ourself more vulnerable, draws out the divine in both of us.

Sometimes I am amazed at the power of a simple and kind expression I give to Joyce. Her face can light up in joy with just a few loving words from me. If I want to give her a great gift, I explore ways to express the beauty I see in her soul at any moment, or I humbly ask her for help with something that has been troubling me. One way, I am a God giving to a Goddess. The other way, I am a God opening to receive from a Goddess. Loving, we are all Gods and Goddesses. Loving, each one of us embraces the divine.

Joyce and I want to live and love as fully as possible and sincerely hope we are never tempted to stop in a comfortable but unfinished stage of growth. We are committed to embrace the soul mirror, within and without, to unite our hearts in the perfection of love, and to allow this union and love to bless others. We encourage every one of you also to live and love as fully as possible—to live from the heart.

List of Practices

Acknowledgments

OUR FAMILY AND FRIENDS HAVE ENCOURAGED US EVERY STEP of the way in the writing and publishing of *The Heart's Wisdom*. We greatly appreciate their support.

We also wish to express our gratitude to the following persons without whose help this book would not have been possible:

Our deepest thanks go to Pat Stacey, master editor and shaper of books from crude raw material. Her dedication allowed her to "live" this book, to work on it night and day, to wake up in the middle of the night with an idea to make it better.

And to Mary Jane Ryan and the dedicated staff of Conari Press, whose vision of a better world goes into every page of this and every book they put out.

We thank our other editors who volunteered long hours helping us to improve this book: Jim Lipson, Paul and May Dawes, Lunaea Weatherstone Hougland, Bernadette and Robert Pambianco-Fudge, and Devayani Smith.

We are grateful for our assistant, Paris Morgan, who entered the handwritten parts of the manuscript onto the computer, and held down the office front so we could be free to work on this book.

About the Authors

JOYCE AND BARRY VISSELL HAVE BEEN A COUPLE SINCE 1964. A nurse and medical doctor/psychiatrist, their main interest since 1972 has been counseling and teaching. As a result of the worldwide interest in their books, they travel internationally conducting talks and workshops on relationship, parenting, and healing. They are the founders and directors of the Shared Heart Foundation, a nonprofit organization dedicated to the healing and well-being of individuals, couples, and families. They live with their three children, Rami, Mira, and John-Nuriel, four Golden Retrievers, five cats, and one horse at their home and center on a hilltop near Santa Cruz, California, where they counsel individuals and couples and offer classes, workshops, and training programs.

OTHER BOOKS AND TAPES BY
JOYCE AND BARRY VISSELL INCLUDE:

The Shared Heart: Relationship Initiations and Celebrations
Models of Love: The Parent-Child Journey
Risk to Be Healed: The Heart of Personal and Relationship Growth
The Shared Heart Experience (two-hour video workshop)

Shared Heart Cards (oracle card set)
Four Paths to the Heart (audio)
The Shared Heart Tape: The Relationship Of Love (audio)
Journey of Love: Couples Moving into Parenthood (audio)
Mother-Child Bonding during Pregnancy (audio)
Transitions into Fatherhood: Personal Growth for Expectant Fathers (audio)

AND BY THEIR DAUGHTER, RAMI:

Rami's Book: The Inner Life of a Child

Joyce and Barry Vissell write a monthly article, "New Dimensions of Relationship," for thirty newspapers and magazines nationwide. It covers many timely topics about relationship and spirituality that have not been addressed in their books.

For more information about the work of the Vissells or the Shared Heart Foundation, you can receive a free (twice yearly) newsletter from them, including information about workshops or events with them to be held in your area, and more information about their books, video workshop, and audiotapes. Or if you would like to sponsor or organize such an event, they may be contacted through:

The Shared Heart Foundation
P. O. Box 2140
Aptos, California 95001
1-800-766-0629 (or locally 831-684-2299)
E-mail: Sharedhf@cruzio.com
www.sharedheart.base.org

Conari Press, established in 1987, publishes books on topics ranging from psychology, spirituality, and women's history to sexuality, parenting, and personal growth. Our main goal is to publish quality books that will make a difference in people's lives—both how we feel about ourselves and how we relate to one another.

Our readers are our most important resource, and we value your input, suggestions, and ideas. We'd love to hear from you—after all, we are publishing books for you!

To request our latest book catalog, or to be added to our mailing list, please contact:

CONARI PRESS
2550 Ninth Street, Suite 101
Berkeley, California 94710-2551
800-685-9595 510-649-7175
fax: 510-649-7190
e-mail: Conari@conari.com
www.conari.com